Indie With Ease

Pauline Wiles is the author of three romantic comedies, including *Saving Saffron Sweeting*, which reached the quarter final in the Amazon Breakthrough Novel Award, a compilation of short stories, and *Indie With Ease*, a self-help guide for self-published authors. Other work has been published by *Toasted Cheese Literary Journal*, *House of Fifty*, and *Alfie Dog Fiction*.

British by birth, she is now a contented resident of California, although she admits to an occasional yearning for afternoon tea and historic homes.

Find her on Twitter @paulinewiles and get more tips on productivity for authors at www.paulinewiles.com/writers

Indie With Ease

Pauline Wiles

Copyright © Pauline Wiles 2018

All rights reserved. No part of this publication may be reproduced, stored in a retrieval system, or transmitted in any form or by any means without prior written permission of the author, nor be otherwise circulated in any form of binding or cover other than that in which it is published and without similar condition being imposed on the purchaser.

ISBN-13: 978-0-9889731-6-9

Contents

Introduction..1
Part 1: Hold Up a Mirror...7
  Chapter 1: Know Yourself.....................................9
  Chapter 2: Assess Your Resources......................15
  Chapter 3: Your Long-Term Aspirations..............20
Part 2: Get Your Ducks in a Row............................31
  Chapter 4: Get Organized....................................33
  Chapter 5: Productivity.......................................46
  Chapter 6: Hone Your Craft................................58
  Chapter 7: Build Your Tribe................................68
  Chapter 8: Nurture Your Creativity.....................73
Part 3: Finesse Your Process..................................87
  Chapter 9: Balance Life With Writing.................89
  Chapter 10: Dealing With Feeling Overwhelmed........97
  Chapter 11: Minimum Viable Product...............103
  Chapter 12: Minimum Viable Marketing...........115
Part 4: Stay Inspired...129
  Chapter 13: The Easiest Pitfalls to Dodge..........131
  Chapter 14: Things Not to Worry About...........143
  Chapter 15: Keeping Your Spirits Up.................152
Conclusion...161
Resources...163
Bonus Downloads...168
Free Mini Course: Focus for Writers....................169

Acknowledgments

My particular thanks to the authors listed below who were kind enough to contribute their experience and wisdom to this book.

In addition, beta readers Jackie Bouchard, Martha Reynolds, and Fedra Pouideh provided both encouragement and insight which helped me sharpen and clarify my message.

Special thanks to Wendy Janes for her sharp-eyed proofreading and further editorial comments. Any remaining errors in the text are mine.

And as usual, my husband Darius provided equal parts technical support and moral support, adding immensely to the *ease* of my writing life.

Sincere Thanks to These Author Contributors:

- Melissa Addey: Historical fiction & nonfiction, https://www.melissaaddey.com/

- Grace Allison Blair: Self-help, http://modernmysticmedia.com/

- Jackie Bouchard: Fido-friendly fiction, http://jackiebouchard.com/

- Pamela Olivia Brown: Paranormal fiction, http://pamelaobrown.com/

- Elizabeth Ducie: Thrillers, short stories & nonfiction, http://elizabethducieauthor.co.uk

- Pat Edwards: Self-help, https://exploringthemagicherosjourney.com/

- Tracey Gemmell: Fiction, https://traceygemmell.com/

- Sue Johnson: Poetry, fiction & nonfiction, http://www.writers-toolkit.co.uk/

- Wendy Janes: Fiction, http://wendyproof.co.uk/published-works/

- Cat Lavoie: Chick Lit, https://www.catlavoie.com/

- Elizabeth Lovick: Nonfiction (crafts), http://www.northernlacepress.co.uk/

- Martha Reynolds: Women's fiction, https://marthareynoldswrites.com/

- Alina Sayre: Fantasy, ages 9–14, https://alinasayre.com/

- Stefania Shaffer: Nonfiction, middle grade fiction, http://stefaniashaffer.com/

- Heather Wardell: Women's fiction, http://heatherwardell.com/

INDIE WITH EASE

Introduction

Today it is easier than ever to publish a book and share your words with the world. If you are determined to see your sentences in print (or on-screen), then the traditional gatekeepers are powerless to prevent you. The joy of holding your book in your hands is truly yours for the taking.

What's more, revenue for book publishers is growing: the Association of American Publishers reported a 6.2% increase in the first quarter of 2018 compared with the previous year. After all, your hard work can now be financially rewarded by readers borrowing ebooks and audiobooks, as well as purchasing copies in electronic and print format. And with the USA accounting for only 29% of global book sales by revenue, a 2017 study by BookMap estimated the global book market is now worth a massive 143 billion US dollars.

However, these colossal numbers indicate you're not the only one who is proud to publish. In fact, hundreds of thousands of authors feel the same way. Worldwide, more books are being released than ever before—upward of a million titles each year. And while hordes of voracious readers are undoubtedly out there, getting your work in front of them is no picnic. After the immense effort of writing your book and hustling to make it available for sale, you might be one of legions of authors who are surprised to find themselves underappreciated and overfatigued.

In my recent survey of self-published authors, over 80% reported feeling stressed and overwhelmed about their writing business. This statistic weighed on my mind, because I'm convinced the pleasure of writing and publishing should be magnified by choosing the independent path, not diminished.

So, in *Indie With Ease*, I share lessons from both myself and 15 other authors on how you can write, publish, and market your work without losing your marbles. This is not another self-publishing how-to, but instead a guide to your well-being, productivity, and serenity as an indie author.

Who is This Book For?

This book is for you if:
- You're early in your author career but are reasonably convinced that independent publishing is your path.
- You are already an independently published author, but you're suffering from fatigue, stress, or disillusionment.
- You want your self-publishing journey to be both enjoyable *and* productive.

It's not for you if:
- You are seeking a traditional publishing deal.
- You're looking for a nuts and bolts guide to the steps and tasks involved in the mechanics of publishing.

There are many (*many*) books on the market that cover the laundry list of tools and services for self-publishers, or claim to offer writing shortcuts and marketing strategies to generate life-changing income. This book offers you something new: practical ways to conquer stress, boost productivity, and love your self-publishing career.

My Quest for Ease

As an indie author myself, with over a quarter of a million words published, I've had my share of ups and downs. But I firmly believe being an author should be a delight, not a drudgery. In my six years in the publishing business I've learned to set realistic expectations, focus doggedly on only the important tasks, and take care of my energy, creativity, and morale.

I began writing fiction seriously in 2012 after I left a job at a startup company which was destroying my *joie de vivre*. Deciding to take a little time off before seeking further employment, I wanted something tangible to show for my sabbatical. Knowing that I couldn't stay home indefinitely, I was determined to publish my novel before heading back to work. As a result, I spurned the lengthy timescales of traditional publishing and threw myself into the indie model without ever seeking an agent or a book deal. *Saving Saffron Sweeting* (a romantic comedy set in my native England) was published early in 2013 and reached the quarter finals of that year's Amazon Breakthrough Novel Award.

Spoiler alert: the income from that first novel was not enough to support me! (If you bought this book hoping to hear otherwise, please seek your refund now and there'll be no hard feelings.) I returned to employment and managed to release two further novels and a collection of short stories.

However, the constant juggling of day job, writing, hobbies, and side projects slowly accumulated to the point where feeling overwhelmed became my steady state. I realized that the glee of writing and publishing was in serious danger of turning to grind. So, for the whole of 2017 I devoted myself to experiments with my mindset, techniques, and habits. My aim was to learn to juggle responsibilities, reduce stress, quiet my mind, and approach rose-smelling serenity. Naturally, I'm still a work in progress, but I'm now convinced that pragmatic self-care and purposeful productivity are the foundations of a long and happy writing career.

And I'm on a mission to help other authors benefit from what I've learned.

How to Use This Book

The chapters in this book are laid out to introduce you to indie author challenges roughly in the order you'll encounter them, but it does not seek to be a step-by-step guide. Feel free to dip into sections which especially interest you, and return to others as you need them.

However, I strongly recommend you read at least Chapters 1, 2, and 3 before diving into the later material. These chapters guide you in the essential self-knowledge of who you are and what you want from this journey, and they provide the reference point and foundation for all your subsequent reading.

Each chapter concludes with self-reflection questions. I encourage you to take the time to consider your answers carefully and to make notes as appropriate. Because every author is different, it's important that you take the advice in each chapter and distill from it the parts which are right for your personality and your situation. There is no one-size-fits-all approach to the author life; the self-reflection questions help you identify your unique needs and action points.

Bonus Downloads

Throughout this book, I refer to additional resources which you can download for free by visiting:

www.paulinewiles.com/indie-with-ease-bonus

These bonus downloads include a workbook for your answers to the self-reflection questions, as well as printable trackers and planners. You'll also find examples, templates, and checklists which I use for my own writing.

The last part of this book includes links to all websites mentioned and suggested further reading. Also, please refer to the acknowledgments pages for a listing of the authors who were kind enough to contribute their wisdom to these chapters. I sincerely hope you'll visit their websites and learn more about their individual author journeys.

Please Get in Touch

I would love to hear your reactions to this book and your insights from your own writing odyssey. Naturally I'd love for you to leave an online review of what you read here, but more than that, I would be delighted to hear from you by email with questions or reactions you'd like to share. You can reach me by email: web@paulinewiles.com, or find me on Twitter: @paulinewiles

Part 1: Hold Up a Mirror

Chapter 1: Know Yourself

To succeed as an indie author, you'll need to know yourself well. If you write fiction, this means digging even deeper into your own character than you do for the people who populate your pages. Self-awareness is the key not only to getting your book written in the first place, but also to weathering the inevitable ups and downs of your chosen path. Knowing your personality type and individual preferences will help you enjoy your journey and move toward a destination you find satisfying.

The following seven questions will help.

How Do You Feel About the Process?

Think about everything that goes into producing a book, from first draft through development, editing, early reader feedback, final edits, proofreading, formatting, cover design, advance reviews, publication, and promotion. Which part(s) of that process excite you most? Which do you dread, or fear? Knowing this gives you insight into the stages of the journey you are likely to enjoy, and where you may struggle. Do you love to switch tasks and welcome variety in your day, or would you prefer to focus on a more narrow skill set?

Jackie Bouchard, who writes what she calls fido-friendly fiction, enjoys the varied process: "Know what you're getting into going it alone... I'm a very detail-oriented person—and a control freak!—so I can self-publish my books fairly cheaply with really only the cover art as an expense. I do my own formatting."

If you love a smörgåsbord of activities, you're well suited to the indie life. If not, don't worry, but that's a signal you should consider getting help for more tasks. Bouchard agrees: "If you don't like fiddling with details, you'll likely need to hire an editor, a formatter, a cover artist."

Are You a Lark or an Owl?

Before you can call yourself an indie author, you have to write a book. And knowing what time of day your energy is highest will be key to your productivity. If you're sharpest between 7AM and 11AM, but you start your day job at 8AM, you have to plan how you'll get around that. If the bulk of your freedom is between 9PM and bedtime, but you can hardly keep your eyes open long enough to brush your teeth, don't plan on getting your best writing done then. You'll either have to renegotiate how your life is currently arranged, or set yourself steadier, gentler targets in line with your realistic energy resources.

If you don't already know whether you're a lark, an owl, or somewhere in between, simply try writing at different times of day and see how it feels, what quantity of work you produce, and what quality. Make a note of your preference, as we'll discuss action steps for planning your day in Chapter 4, and harnessing your energy in Chapter 9.

You can find a writing tracker in the free bonus downloads which accompany this book: www.paulinewiles.com/indie-with-ease-bonus

Are You More Extrovert or Introvert?

If you're an extrovert trying to write a nonfiction how-to guide, you might find meeting and interviewing your subjects far easier than solo, online research. If you're an introvert, you might not thrive in a boisterous writers' group where everyone is expected to read aloud and then deal with instant critique.

When it comes to promotion, knowing your preference for being around people will influence which methods come most naturally to you. There's a world of difference between writing a guest post for a blog, and hosting a booth at a trade show.

Fiction author Tracey Gemmell adds, "Most of us in this business are introverts. Marketing ourselves can be excruciating. There's no way around it. We must study the art of marketing as closely as we study the art of writing if we want to survive."

If you don't already know where you fall on the introvert/extrovert spectrum, a great question to consider is, do you feel refreshed and recharged from being around people, or do you replenish your energy levels best from being alone? Being an introvert is not the same as being shy, or being antisocial. It's more a case of how you derive energy. At the end of a long working week, do you gravitate to a night out with others, or a night in alone?

Your preference on the introvert/extrovert spectrum will guide you in creating accountability (Chapter 5), building your tribe (Chapter 7), and your natural marketing tactics (Chapter 12).

How Do You Respond to Expectations?

Bestselling author Gretchen Rubin has a highly informative framework for how we each react to expectations coming from ourselves and from others. In her book, *The Four Tendencies*, she names: Upholder, Obliger, Questioner, and Rebel. For example, if you're an Obliger (the biggest group), you'll likely need a high degree of *external accountability* in order to meet your goals. A writing buddy or accountability partner, who will check on your progress regularly, might be perfect for you.

You can find your tendency by taking Rubin's free assessment, see *The Four Tendencies* in Website References at the end of this book. Then review the resources on that site to learn more about how best to meet your expectation of becoming a published author.

Are You a Plotter or a Pantser?

These charming terms refer to a preference to plan and outline a novel, versus the freewheeling approach of just jumping in and writing. If you're a plotter, you'll struggle to complete a writing project without a route map. If you're a pantser, you'll feel bored or stifled by knowing in advance where your characters and plot are heading.

If you can't already sense your preference, why not try both methods for a short writing project, and see how it feels? Alternatively, National Novel Writing Month (NaNoWriMo), an annual effort where writers attempt to draft a 50,000-word novel in just 30 days, has great resources. See National Novel Writing Month in the Website References at the end of this book.

Where Do You Write Best?

Countless writers report they can't get anything done at home, preferring instead to leave their domestic surroundings in favor of coffee shops, libraries, laundromats, and trains. My productivity, on the other hand, plummets in a café, where I devote at least 40% of my time to refilling my tea and subsequently exploring the restroom.

Self-help author Pat Edwards found a regular lunchtime spot to blend writing with her other job: "I left my desk and went to a private phone space. I set a timer and I stopped when the timer went off. I didn't judge or edit, I just spewed as much as I could in the allotted time."

If you don't already know your best venue, just visit a selection of places, write for an hour, and prepare to be surprised. Just remember to keep your laptop under close guard, for example, locking it to a table when you step away for a moment. And before you leave home to work somewhere else, make sure to back up your work.

You'll find a writing tracker in the bonus downloads, to help you experiment with different locations. Chapter 5 will help you build on this self-knowledge.

What Are You Willing to Sacrifice?

It takes hundreds of hours to write and publish a book. Few, if any, of us have time like that lying around, so you need to get honest about what you're willing to give up or cut back. Examples include:
- Television
- Social media
- Laundry for your teenage kids
- Volunteering
- Outings with friends
- Sunday with the in-laws
- Sporting events
- Browsing at the mall
- Computer games
- Friday night at the pub
- Cooking from scratch
- Ironing sheets
- Weekend naps

At the same time, consider what you are absolutely *not* willing to give up. Depending on what's a firm priority for you, this might be sport with your kids, date night with your beloved, or sleep. We'll talk more about the importance of sleep in Chapter 8. For now, know that the timeworn advice to wake up earlier to write your book simply doesn't work *unless* you compensate in the evening by going to bed earlier. Don't let anyone convince you to put your health at risk by stealing from sleep on an ongoing basis.

As you work through the sections on Productivity (in Chapter 5) and Pitfalls (in Chapter 13), refer back to this list of activities you may be willing to reduce. It will nudge you to notice where you're spending your time and where your priorities really lie.

Summary

As an indie author you'll encounter endless advice about how to write and publish your work. Knowing what works for *you*, and what doesn't, is invaluable in helping you filter and apply that advice. Don't be afraid to carve out your own methods and reject approaches which others swear by. Spending a little time studying your own preferences will boost not only your productivity but your happiness in other areas of your life.

By now you should know your feelings on:
- Parts of the process you'll love, or hate.
- Lark or owl.
- Extrovert or introvert.
- Upholder, Obliger, Questioner, or Rebel.
- Plotter or pantser.
- Best writing location.
- Activities to sacrifice or hold sacred.

Self-Reflection Questions

1) What have you learned about yourself from the topics and personality types discussed in this chapter?

2) What surprises did you encounter when considering your own character nuances?

3) How will you change your writing habits as a result?

Chapter 2: Assess Your Resources

Imagine for a moment you are planning to build your own home. You don't just want to pitch a tent or throw a tin roof over a few bricks: you want to create a quality structure which is attractive, practical, and lasts. Since there are so many facets to this complex project, the more time, skills, tenacity, and experienced friends you have, the easier it will be.

Indie publishing is similar: if you're seriously considering this path, you're potentially preparing to wear many different hats, and/or to pull in a variety of resources.

Your Time

Don't make the mistake of thinking you can't succeed as an indie author without a lot of time. You can: you'll just need to slow your process down, consider finding help for more parts, and allow more elapsed time for each book release.

Look back at what you said you were willing to give up in Chapter 1, look at your schedule and other commitments, and make a realistic estimate of how much time you can spend on your writing life. This will encompass not just the actual writing, but all the other accompanying tasks too.

Skills

If you've tried a lot of different jobs, failed to specialize in much, and never quite felt you cracked the problem of what to do when you grew up, congratulations, you might be ideally suited to be an indie author. If you've tinkered around with websites, grappled with Microsoft Word documents, dabbled in Google analytics, or flicked through a graphic design magazine, so much the better. Take an honest look at your skills, and don't be hard on yourself: you'd be surprised what comes in handy as an indie author. At a minimum, I hope you will identify writing skills, and that you love to read!

Elizabeth Lovick, whose niche is knitting Shetland lace, decided she could add the skill of self-publishing to her other crafting accomplishments: "I fell in to publishing, rather than planned it. We had a book in the making, and several companies wanted to publish it. They said it would take two years. We wanted it out (in) five months' time. I researched online and reckoned we could do it ourselves."

Next, look at trusted friends and close family: people you can count on to actually deliver, if they agree to help you. Is anyone particularly good with computers, design, marketing, PR, project management, or data analysis? Good: get ready to harness them. Do you know any published authors (whether traditional or indie)? Great: they'll have loads of tips.

You do, of course, need to be a little cautious when inviting your nearest and dearest to help in your author journey. Even if they wholeheartedly agree this is a great project for you, they may have inflated opinions of the skills they bring. They may not deliver top quality work and they likely won't consider their deliverables as much of a priority as you do. It's awkward enough if you're paying someone, but if you hate the (no cost) Gothic cover your nephew comes up with for your contemporary romance, you'll be in a tough position. As another example, it's rare to have a qualified, experienced proofreader in your circle of acquaintances. If you do, terrific, but don't let a detail-oriented friend who's an avid reader be your only source of error checking.

If you can't pull together website help, document formatting, and graphic design from people who'll work for you for free, know that you'll likely end up paying for these services. So, in addition, take a look at your professional contacts for people who truly excel in these areas. You'll need to check if they're available, affordable, and will deliver as agreed.

There are plenty of authors who only want to write, and I understand and admire that single-minded focus. However, my sense from indie authors I meet is that they are more likely to be willing to turn their hand to related tasks. In order to self-publish with any degree of success, you're either nimble enough to pick up a few new skills, or you have to be prepared to pay for help at every step of the way. There's no right or wrong approach, but the former will be kinder on your bank balance.

Body of Work

What work do you have that's currently unpublished, or previously published but the rights have reverted back to you? Many writers have a myriad of projects started but not finished, or which are complete but have not yet found an audience. Review these assets: you'd be surprised how much collateral you have which could be polished and published. You might not have entire books lying around, but you could pull bonus material, blog posts, or guest articles from your pile.

Your Support Network

As well as concrete skills you can use, who from your friends and family will offer moral support and cheerleading? Who could be a mentor, or an accountability partner? Your aunt who's working on a handmade quilt might be a valuable resource to boost your morale, self-belief, and tenacity. Don't overlook the value offered by those who bring positivity to your equation. There will be plenty of times when you need friendly encouragement and to be prodded to keep going.

Later in this book I'll discuss the substantial support which comes from other authors, so it's not too early to start building genuine, thoughtful connections with those whose work you admire, or who are at a similar stage of their author career.

Money

You definitely don't need deep pockets to become an indie author and it's certainly possible these days to release your work to the world without spending a penny. But if you want to publish a *quality* book that provides a pleasant reading experience, you'll need to invest some of your own money. This is even more true if you find you are lacking in time, or skills, or both.

Much has been written about how much it costs to publish a book and it's beyond my scope here to suggest a budget for your own particular circumstances. But you'll likely need to pay for proofreading, cover design, and an ISBN number, *at a minimum*. I spent around $1000 on publishing my first novel. Compared to many authors, this was definitely on the low side.

Tracey Gemmell noticed the process was costly, too: "I knew making a living writing would be difficult. I didn't realize even covering self-publishing costs would be a major accomplishment."

Summary

Hopefully the review of your resources has left you pleasantly surprised by the many assets available to you in your author journey. There are so many aspects of bringing a book to life and reaching readers, one of your key tasks will be to harness both your own energy and that of others. Don't forget to look for help in unlikely places, remember that assistance can be both free and paid, and you may find unexpected enjoyment in the new skills you acquire along the way.

Equally, if you feel your resources are lacking in some areas, don't spend time now worrying about your weak points. As you move through your author journey, you'll get a better sense of which holes need to be plugged and how you'll do that. In particular, don't use a perceived lack of resources as a reason to put your author dream to one side. You can find a way around your obstacles, when you reach them.

Self-Reflection Questions

1) What resources did you identify which will help your author aspirations? List them under the following headings: Time; Skills; Body of Work; Support; Money.

2) In which areas do you suspect resources are a little lacking? Note these and move on.

3) Which relationships could you invest time in now, so that you feel more comfortable asking for support in the future? For example, family, friends, other writers.

Chapter 3: Your Long-Term Aspirations

Please don't go a single step further in your indie author career without stopping to consider your long-term aspirations. You can't navigate this journey with peace and ease until you're clear on what success looks like *for you*. Your definition of achievement may look dramatically different from someone else's and there's simply no point pursuing a dream which isn't your own.

First, why are you publishing? Do you want to entertain, enlighten, educate, enable, or empower your readers? Should they end up feeling informed, or comforted? Challenged, concerned, or cozy? Outraged, or amused?

Will this be your sole book, and once it's out there in the world, you're done? Or do you want to publish multiple times? If you don't know yet, that's okay. But it's helpful to have an idea of whether publishing is a one-time bucket list item, or whether you might continue if you find the process enjoyable and worthwhile.

And what does *worthwhile* even mean? Will you measure your success financially, or in terms of readers reached? Does accomplishment, for you, mean a signing event in a large bookstore? Or does it simply mean everyone in your extended family receives their own copy of the precious information you need to share? You might even feel you've reached your personal finish line when you hold your book in your hands, or see it available for sale online.

I asked several indie authors about their hopes and expectations. One of them was Alina Sayre, who writes fantasy novels for ages 9–14. She says, "I think it's important to know why you write. I didn't get into writing to become rich or famous, which is good, because I haven't! Basically, I write because I love to write, and because I believe stories can change the world. I'm constantly reexamining my balance of long-term and short-term goals, always trying to find ways to pay the bills while still preserving some space for writing in my life."

Rank These Achievements

To get clear on what you're striving for, consider this list of achievements and rank them in order of importance to you:
- Seeing your book in a bookstore.
- Seeing your book in an airport store.
- Holding your book in your hands.
- Throwing a book launch party.
- Visiting a book club to talk about your work.
- Seeing yourself on Amazon next to a bestseller in your genre.
- Seeing yourself on Amazon, at any sales rank.
- Making the *New York Times* (or similar) bestseller list.
- Receiving a five-star online review from an acquaintance.
- Receiving a five-star online review from a stranger.
- Selling the movie rights to your book.
- Hearing from a reader that they stayed up past their bedtime with your book.
- Hearing from a reader that you changed their life.

Your approach to your author life should be different, according to your aspirations.

In his book, *The Mindful Writer*, Dinty W. Moore warns, "Many people want to be writers because they imagine it is a life of breezy cocktail parties, triumphant book tours, jovial fan mail, and endless champagne and caviar." Instead, he believes, "Doing something—writing, for instance—not for money, not for fame, not for lording your achievements over others, but for the joy of it, the exhilaration, is not just the proper way to act, but it is what will best sustain you."

It's fine for goals to evolve as you learn more about yourself as a writer and conditions in the industry, but try to have some initial idea of what would feel like success to you. That way, you can avoid getting caught up in chasing an outcome which isn't satisfying. And even if you would enjoy all the things listed above, knowing how they rank in importance will be key in helping you prioritize where to spend scarce time and resources.

Women's fiction author Martha Reynolds agrees that her aspirations have adjusted along the way. "Seven novels and nearly six years later, my expectations are, I suppose, more realistic. I have *not* been offered a traditional publishing deal, and I have *not* earned enough from sales to live self-sufficiently. But I write novels because I enjoy it, and because I've now got lots of loyal readers who tell me they can't wait for my next book."

Your aspirations might also be an indication of whether you are likely to be truly happy as an indie author. If, from the list above, you ranked seeing your book in an airport store or selling movie rights close to the top, please take particular note of the next section.

Do You Really Want to Be Indie?

Talking of dreams, if, deep down, you're yearning for a traditional book deal, a self-guided author career may frustrate you and leave you feeling like you've settled.

Do any of the following apply to you?
1. For as long as you can remember, you've wanted to see your book in a bookstore.
2. You want a big name publisher on the spine of your book.
3. You've already drawn up a detailed cast list for who should play your characters in a movie.

4. You can't imagine navigating editing, cover design, publication, and distribution without expert help.
5. You believe professionals will make better decisions about editing, cover design, and pricing than you would.
6. You'd like the validation of knowing your book is "good enough" to be traditionally published.
7. Your family, or others who are important to you, don't think it "counts" if you self-publish.
8. You don't mind waiting as long as it takes to see your work in the world.
9. You believe self-published books are poor quality.
10. You just want to write, and let someone else handle marketing.

If you answered *Yes* for any of the first eight points, you may not be mentally ready to set sail as an indie author. Everyone's circumstances are different and whichever path (traditional or indie) you choose, you may wonder what the other would have held. However, those first eight points are signs your heart may not be ready to embrace the joy of being indie.

To be clear, I'm definitely *not* saying that traditional forms of success, like seeing your book in a store, are out of reach for indie authors. You *can* get your book into shops and you *can* get validation from esteemed sources. However, those eight beliefs are clues to your feelings about self-publishing.

The ninth point, that self-published books are necessarily poor quality, is a false assumption. Of course, there are many cringe-worthy indie books released every day and I concur there are more likely to be quality issues with independently published work. But it is perfectly possible to produce beautiful, high quality books as an indie, and I suggest you set your sights on no less.

What about the last point above? Here's the brutal truth about today's publishing world: to sell lots of copies, you need to be prepared to hurl yourself into marketing—*lots* of marketing—regardless who publishes your work. This doesn't apply to authors seeking to share a highly personal book with only their nearest and dearest. But for everyone else, you must embrace promotional tasks. The days of a publisher handling all that for you are long gone. Jackie Bouchard says, "My author pals who have worked with New York publishers spent significant amounts of their own money on PR, and some admitted to me they didn't even earn out their advances. Once you don't earn out your advance, they're even less likely to give you much support for your next book, and then it's kind of a vicious cycle..."

So, you are your Chief Marketing Officer, and while that doesn't mean you have to do everything yourself, never assume that a book deal means someone else will promote your book without your involvement.

As already mentioned, I opted for the indie author route right out of the gate. However, many indie authors come to this method *after* trying to land an agent and publisher. There are compelling reasons for that sequential approach and I'm not here to bash you for trying. But do know that at the point you decide to take the indie option, you should feel happy and excited about that decision. Don't read this book feeling like you've settled for second best. Much like choosing a partner in life, *settling* isn't a recipe for long-lasting ease.

Take the time you need to get comfortable with your choice, and don't try to force an acceptance you don't yet feel. Pamela Olivia Brown, who writes paranormal fiction, remembers, "My decision to publish independently was easy, but I procrastinated for years. As soon as I hit the 'submit' button for my haiku chapbook, I was pleasantly surprised at how easy it was. I felt that everyone should self-publish."

Let's assume you've made your peace with taking the driving seat as an independent author. And you have already considered your personality (Chapter 1) and resources (Chapter 2) which help inform what approaches are likely to be realistic for you. So it's time to consider another important aspiration.

What Are Your Financial Expectations?

If you picked up this book hoping for an easy path to writerly riches, then sorry, I'm not here to deliver that. You can't lose 20 pounds in a week, you can't run a marathon with ten days' training, and it's my firm belief that first-time indie authors are highly unlikely to strike it rich. At this point, let's pause and remember I'm British: it's in my nature to take a cautious view, and my cheerleading style is muted at best. Yes, you might find astounding success with your first book and you might have a commercial hit on your hands. But since my mission here is to protect your well-being, I'd be doing you a disservice to imply that massive sales as an indie author are probable. *Possible*, yes, but not probable.

Consider the goal of breaking even on your book. For a first-time author, this seems like a reasonable aim, and it's the one I set for my first novel, *Saving Saffron Sweeting*. However, widely quoted statistics suggest the average self-published book sells just 250 copies in its lifetime. Depending on the costs you incur, that's unlikely to put you in the black with your book efforts. Meanwhile, Brooke Warner, publisher at She Writes Press, says that selling 1000 copies signals a reasonably successful book. Would that be enough? If you spent $1000 like I did, and priced your ebook at $2.99, then, yes, you will probably break even. But keep in mind that number of copies means your book is well received and selling way more than most.

Multiple conversations with other indie authors tell me the vast majority are in the business because they love to write and publish, not to become wealthy, or even pay the mortgage. For many, actually, their writing doesn't even pay the electricity bill. I've had plenty of months where my books bring in four-figure revenue. But I've had many more months where my writing pays for about a dozen foamy drinks at Starbucks. Jackie Bouchard is equally pragmatic: "You have to do this because you love the process. Don't get into writing with the goal of making it rich. It's a nice dream to have in the background, but it's not an easy way to make a living, let alone get rich."

To be clear, I'm not saying you *can't* make big bucks with your writing. Just know that it's highly unlikely, at least at first. As you build readership and your books earn online reviews, it gets a little easier. In fact, author earnings are strongly correlated with how many books they have published. For example, promoting your book through limited-time special pricing is more effective if you have more than one title published: the attention drawn to one will boost the others too. Survey after survey shows that the indie authors making the most money are the ones who've written multiple books.

In other words, it truly is a marathon, not a sprint. If your long-term aspiration is to publish one time and take delight in that achievement, that's fine. But if you've got your sights on earning a living (or even paying a chunk of your bills), you'd be well advised to anticipate a longer runway. Unfortunately there's no magic formula for the number of books an indie author publishes before the money picks up, but the more work you produce, the more efficient you'll get at both writing and publishing. In addition, your sense of which promotional methods work best for you will flourish too.

Do you have a day job? For goodness' sake, keep it. I repeat: *do not give up your main source of income* until you've been through the indie publishing loop at least once and know what realistic earnings look like for you. Alternatively, perhaps you have a buffer of savings? Maybe even a partner or family member who is willing to serve as your "patron of the arts"? Tracey Gemmell agrees on the need for caution. She says, "Don't slam the door shut on your day job. Is a leave of absence possible? Is part-time an option? If a writer's life turns out not as you expected, having a Plan B can relieve stress."

I would love for you to prove me wrong with your overnight success, but just to be safe, nurture another source of income in addition to your writing.

I'm sorry if this is depressing and it's certainly not intended to be defeatist. There are so many joys in writing and publishing your own book(s), you can and should measure your returns more widely than money. But, for most of us, income matters deeply. This book aims to mitigate your stress and guide you on an enjoyable journey, so I'm spelling out these monetary truths because financial disillusionment makes for restless nights.

If you'd like to see further research and extensive statistics on how much authors really make from their books, the Author Earnings website is an excellent and up-to-date resource: see Website References at the end of this book.

Write What You Love

While we're on the topic of aspirations, and having delivered a reality check about getting rich as an author, I want to warn against the temptation to write on a subject because you believe it will be commercially lucrative.

Remember the vampire rush of a few years ago? How about the more recent decluttering craze? Unlike traditional publishing, where timelines between writing and launch are usually lengthy, we indies are well positioned to identify a mainstream demand and hustle to write something which fits. Unless you're an extraordinarily fast writer and the topic is a close fit to your existing interests, please resist this urge. Here are five good reasons why:

1. It's far too hard to predict where trends will go. And although a little competition is a good thing, being one of dozens of books on that topic suddenly

flooding virtual shelves won't help establish your niche.
2. You'll come across as (and feel) more authentic if you stick to what you love. Readers will sense whether your heart is truly in it.
3. You'll find it much easier to sustain your efforts for the long haul. Writing and publishing your book will demand a large proportion of your waking hours, so be sure to spend that time in the company of words you actually like.
4. Your work will be better: if you love a genre or type of book, you know the norms which readers expect and the stereotypes to avoid. Simply put, you're more able to write the kind of book you yourself are longing to read.
5. Building your support network in the author community will be considerably breezier if the writers you connect with are truly your tribe. Again, authenticity counts.

The Swedish Concept of *Lagom*

I was tempted to mention *lagom* in the financial goals section, but this Swedish word embraces far more than that. Meaning *just the right amount*, I encourage you to think about *lagom* in the context of your writing. What does *not too little, but not too much* mean to you? How much time should your indie author activities occupy? How many words or books should you produce? How much recognition would be just right, and how much income would be a *lagom* amount for you? *Lagom* represents moderation and balance, not extreme or excess.

And Tracey Gemmell, whose fiction covers themes of what truly makes for a satisfying life, offers this perspective: "Do you love writing or are you in love with the idea of writing, of breaking out of the box you're currently in? The answer to this question is vital if you're to survive long-term as an author."

It's my firm belief you will thrive as an indie if you aim for *lagom* in your activities and aspirations. For more information, try reading *Lagom: Not Too Little, Not Too Much* by Niki Brantmark.

Summary

Being sure that you are comfortable with the decision to publish independently, and knowing a few ideal outcomes for your work, will be a big help as you start to navigate your author journey.

Meanwhile, setting realistic financial expectations will help you guard against disillusionment and early burnout. Employ the principle of *not too little, not too much* in your writing life, and stay true to what you love to write, to further anchor your sense of purpose and ease.

Self-Reflection Questions

1) What did you note as the top three achievements which are important to you as an author?

2) What's your comfort level with deciding to pursue the independent publishing path? Do you need to question any of your former beliefs or assumptions in order to feel more committed to this choice?

3) What is your financial goal for your first, or next, book?

Part 2: Get Your Ducks in a Row

Chapter 4: Get Organized

Creative individuals often spurn the suggestion of getting organized, fearing they'll be boxed in by rigid expectations. However, it's my belief that many indie authors are adept at using both sides of their brain together, so it's possible you'll welcome the idea of structuring your time, analyzing your task list, and organizing your writing files. Even if you'd prefer to take each day entirely as it comes, know that a little thought and planning can help you make significantly better use of the limited time you have available.

However, as with all the advice in this book, if you don't get benefit from these organizing suggestions, give yourself permission to drop them and move on!

The Weekly Time Block Method

Depending on your personality type, you'll either love or hate the idea of sketching out your entire week and identifying what needs to happen when. The advantage is you get some insight into where your pockets of time lurk, and you can assess whether all the jigsaw pieces of your life really do fit. If you hate this idea, don't force it. But for those of us who love structure and predictability, it can be exceptionally illuminating to draw a weekly schedule of what you would ideally be doing when.

1. Some time management experts recommend tracking your time first to see where it goes, but I prefer an iterative approach where you jump right in with your aspirations and then continually adjust.
2. Make a sketch or spreadsheet with every (waking) hour of every day represented. I love to do this exercise on a big sheet of paper, with small Post-it notes for different activities. If, like me, you really

enjoy purchasing stationery, choose different color Post-its to represent the roles of your life.
3. Fill in your obligations, such as a day job, home and family duties, personal care, and meal times.
4. Fill in your non-negotiables (see Chapter 1) and self-care routines (coming up in Chapter 8). Be sure to leave some time simply for "fun," and ideally a little contingency here and there for life's curve balls.
5. Now identify the times available for your author activities. Shocked how few slots there are? Go back to step 3 and force yourself to think differently. Or, are there plenty of slots, but they're in small time fragments? Again, see if you can tweak your schedule, or refer to the encouragement on fragments in Chapter 9.
6. Split your author time into writing, promotion/community, and skill-building. If you have eight hours a week available for book activities, you might choose to use four for writing, three for promotion and connecting with others, and one for working on your craft or learning a new skill.
7. Adjust your activities so that low-energy tasks sit at times of day when you're tired or less creative. (See section entitled *Are You a Lark or an Owl?* in Chapter 1.) You might, for example, write early in the morning and then spend time on social media, or reading, after dinner.
8. *Do not* steal time from sleep, exercise, or self-care. Even if you plan to get up at 5AM to write, be sure your bedtime shifts accordingly.
9. *Do* negotiate for help, look for tasks you can delegate, and get tough with yourself about how often "repeaters" (see later in this chapter), need to happen.

Even if you love the week-mapping approach, be prepared to be flexible. I've never yet had a week where I've allocated time as scheduled. And after a few weeks, you'll definitely want to adjust as you learn how long things truly take, and whether the balance of writing/promotion/learning works for you.

The Daily Three Things Method

If a weekly time block feels too constraining, try starting each day with a list of just *three things* you want to get done. Keep them clearly defined (tasks, not whole projects) and achievable. At least one of them should move you toward an important writing or personal goal: put a star next to that. For example:
- Write 600 words—starred.
- Take dog to vet.
- Bake cookies with kids.

Hopefully, your day's accomplishments will go far beyond these. But if everything else descends into turmoil, you'll draw encouragement from squeezing those three things in. Aim to take care of the starred item as early in the day as possible. That way, you minimize the chances of emergency diversions, and you'll gain valuable momentum for other tasks too.

A personal breakthrough for me occurred when I started keeping my calendar and my to-do list in the same place. I treated myself to a customized Agendio planner, but I've also found Google Calendar, where you can combine appointments and reminders in one view, equally effective. The key advantage to having both in one view is it will stop you from listing too many to-dos on days when your calendar is simply packed. The important underlying principle, of course, is to avoid adding things to your calendar which are not high value. Since most of us make a to-do list *after* our schedules are planned, there's a risk your low value meetings and appointments will crowd out your important projects. If you sense that's happening, you need to reevaluate what activities you're saying "yes" to (see section entitled *What Are You Willing to Sacrifice?* in Chapter 1) and/or consider the weekly time blocking method.

Repeaters and Completers

If minor tasks, especially those from elsewhere in your life, keep getting in the way of your writing, you might want to stop to assess what's a "repeater" and what's a "completer." I've been unable to determine which productivity guru originally came up with these distinctions, but I've found them incredibly illuminating and ponder them often.

A repeater is a task which, no matter how many times you do it, it will need doing again. Most household chores fall here: laundry, ironing, cleaning, grocery shopping. But so do posting on social media, checking your website analytics and updating your book sales figures.

A completer, on the other hand, is done once, or at least only once in a long period of time. So buying a house, writing your will, or painting your bedroom would all count as completers in my mind. Likewise, buying a domain name, setting up an email newsletter opt-in page, and pressing *publish* for your book are specific, finite tasks.

It's often the case that higher value tasks are completers, while repeaters have less value, but it's not a hard and fast rule. Healthy habits are definitely repeaters, but they clearly move us toward important long-term goals. However, it does seem that many adults find it more rewarding to work on a completer (example: finalize a book cover design) than a repeater (example: do laundry because your toddler threw up again).

So, if you feel you have too much going on, take a careful look at your repeaters. These might be your low value, dispiriting time sucks. And usually, if you delay a repeater, it will wait until you're ready. If you skip pulling weeds in your garden this Saturday, I'm pretty sure they'll be waiting there for you next weekend instead. Many of us set standards for how often a repeater needs to happen but, if we're brutally honest, we could get by with a lower frequency. You might not want to compromise with how often you put fresh sheets on your bed, but perhaps you could get away with only sporadically dusting the tops of your picture frames.

Resource/Benefit Quadrant Chart

This is a simple concept and one you may see applied to many areas of life and business. If you haven't come across it before, see visual examples below. You can also find a completed quadrant chart, plus a blank one for you to use, in the bonus downloads.

In this example, I'm using the method to assess book promotion opportunities. Draw a sketch like the one on the next page, which shows *Resources* on the vertical axis and *Impact on Sales* on the horizontal:

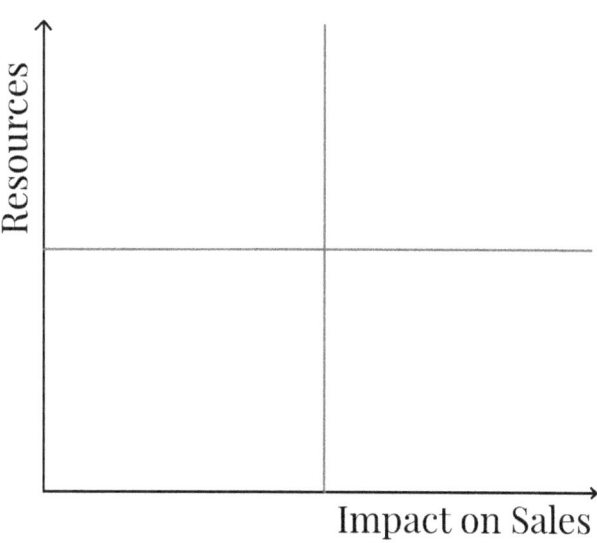

For each book promotion idea I'm considering, I write it on the chart roughly where it belongs in terms of those two aspects. I don't get hung up about exact positions, I just go with a placement which feels reasonable.

Let's say, for example, I want to approach an independent bookstore about an author event. It will take me several hours to land and deliver the gig, but I believe I can generate healthy in-person sales and reader connections as a result. I'd place that one high on both resources and impact:

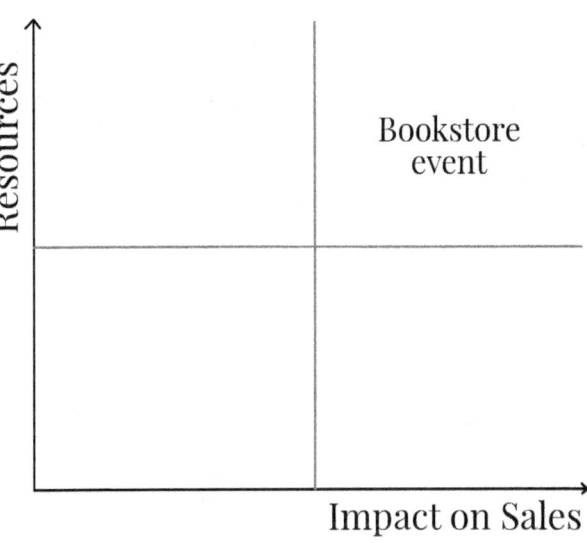

Resources represent both time and money. If, like many authors, both are precious to you, then measure the cost of your efforts as a combination. But, if you have a robust marketing budget and not much time, mark items as high in resources if they consume lots of time, with less consideration of money. And vice versa: if you have next to nothing to spend, but decent time to invest, then costly tactics score higher.

You're unlikely to be able to forecast *Impact on Sales* entirely accurately, and you may be okay with either a short-term sales boost or longer-term awareness building. You can use gut feel here, according to where your ideal readers hang out, the nature of your books, and things you've heard are effective for other authors in your genre.

Don't confuse *reaching people* with *conversion to sales*: a tweet, for example, may be seen by hundreds of eyes, but if they don't buy your book (or take some other valuable action, like subscribing to your email newsletter), the impact is low.

Below, I've filled in the chart with a few example items, using the scenario of an author who writes historical fiction with a strong, local setting. As an extra optional step, you can circle any tasks you'd particularly enjoy:

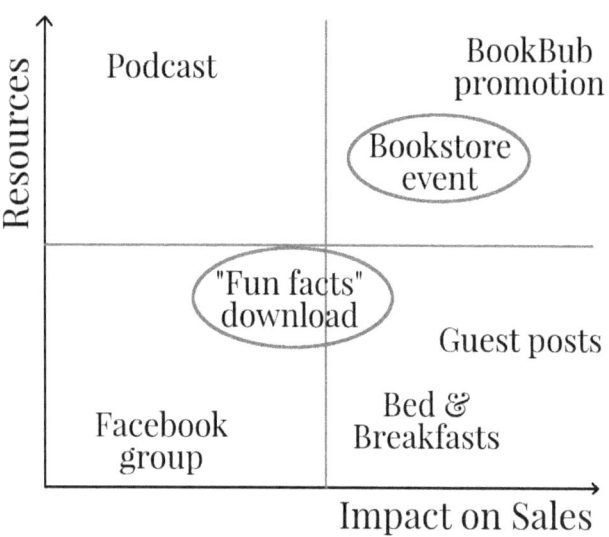

Then pause to consider your quadrants:

High resources, low impact (top left quadrant): *Stay away from these.* Don't invest heavily, if you don't expect a strong outcome.

High resources, high impact (top right quadrant): *Worth considering*, but be sure to measure your results carefully.

Low resources, low impact (bottom left quadrant): *These might be worth pursuing*, especially if you have times when your energy is too low for writing, or if you have a few marketing dollars left at the end of the month. The ideas you circled are particularly worth noting.

Low resources, high impact (bottom right quadrant): *These are your ideal activities to focus on.* If any are circled, even better.

I love this method as it forces me to pause and get realistic about the spectrum of could-dos which float around in my mind. Even if you can't predict outcomes perfectly, you'll still get a meaningful sense of where to spend your time, and reduce your sense of feeling overwhelmed.

Kill Your (Task) Darlings

Nobel Prize laureate William Faulkner famously urged us writers to kill the darlings in our manuscripts, but I have a different darling in mind here.

How often do you make a to-do list? When you do, do you notice any tasks which you persistently transfer from the old list to the new? If you have items you never quite get around to, take a moment to ask yourself if they're *really* important. If you keep delaying them with no apparent consequences, there's a good chance they're not truly necessary. What would happen if you simply scrapped those tasks?

If repeated deferring characterizes your lists, there's also the possibility you've picked a writing goal which just isn't right for you, or is no longer relevant. From time to time, revisit some of the questions in Chapter 3 to see if your heart still truly wants the things you thought. It's perfectly natural for our ambitions to evolve; your creativity and joy will dwindle fast if you feel hog-tied by last year's goals.

If, like me, you have some difficulty letting go of tasks you once thought important, you might want to try a light-hearted ceremony to bid them farewell. Flying Wish Paper is usually used to give wings to hopes, but I've also heard reports that it creates a welcome release when used for freeing yourself of unwanted thoughts. Essentially, you'll write your task on a slip of special paper, and set light to it. Watch as it burns down... and then floats into the air. You should, of course, exercise appropriate caution with matches and flames in your home.

Organize Your Work

With only so many hours in the day, and a fraction of those available for your writing activities, you don't want to waste a single minute looking for information.

I'm one of the most organized people I know, yet I still struggled for years to corral my writing documents. This goes way beyond the materials you need for an individual book, but extends into everything you need to keep your author business orderly.

You can find the overall file structure I now use in the bonus downloads for this book. My high level folders are:
1. Ideas
2. Projects (Current and completed)
3. Technique tips and craft
4. Publishing mechanics
5. Promotion (This contains an eye-watering 21 sub-folders!)
6. Financial

7. Tools (For example, if I'm exploring using Scrivener, I keep tutorials here)
8. Happy Files (See Chapter 15)

My best organizing tips:
- Unless you rely on searching to find emails (I'm too OCD for that), set up the *same* folder structure for emails as for files on your computer.
- Choose a filing method which can be backed up. To decide how often to backup, work out how painful it would be to lose a month's worth of work, or a week, or a day. Your reaction tells you how often you need to safeguard your files. Working on a cloud service like Google Drive, or having automatic backups of your computer files, are excellent options.
- Decide how you'll gather ideas for future work. Many writers use notebooks which are portable and tactile, but these can't be searched and are hard to backup. I've been using Evernote, but may explore other options in future. Try categorizing notes and ideas along these lines:
  - Fiction
    - List of superfluous words to cut
    - Major story ideas
    - Secondary plots, anecdotes
    - Short story prompts
    - Character traits, quirks, interesting hobbies
    - Romantic conflicts, reasons relationships break up
    - Names you'd like to use for characters and places
    - Location or setting notes
  - Nonfiction
    - Sources
    - Quotes

- Research
- Outlines and mind-maps
- Projects you might tackle
- Be sure to keep careful track of ideas you've already used, especially if your indie author ambitions include multiple books. At a minimum, you'll want character sketches of everyone, major *and* minor, so you don't end up with everyone having similar hobbies or taking trips to the same countries. After I'd published three novels I realized I didn't have a good record of tiny details, like cities mentioned in passing, jokes used, and even what food was eaten by whom and when. If your locations repeat, you'll need to make sure they look, sound, and smell consistent from book to book.
- I try to resist keeping a lot of information on paper, but nonetheless some is inevitable. To keep things simple for your brain, start with the same paper files as you have top level folders, and if you need sub-categories, use the same labels as your computer files.

Summary

If organizing your time, papers, and electronic life is one of your favorite hobbies, I hope you'll experiment at length with the different planning methods and task management techniques suggested here.

On the other hand, if you resist encouragement by others to plan and structure your life, then I'd suggest you start with the Daily Three Things Method and see if this adds to your ease. Then, let any further steps evolve as you're ready.

Regardless of your feelings about organizing, I have found the concept of repeaters and completers to be particularly revealing and I hope this helps you view your tasks differently too.

Self-Reflection Questions

1) Have you tried the "time blocking" or "three things" approach to task management? Which one resonates more with you, and what did you learn from your first attempts?

2) Take a look at the current to-dos on your list or in your head. Which of these are completers, and which could be classed as repeaters?

3) Did you identify any "task darlings" you plan to kill? Does a Flying Wish Paper ceremony appeal to you?

Chapter 5: Productivity

Much of the advice on succeeding as an indie author asserts that being prolific is important for commercial visibility and success. Clearly, high productivity is a key factor in being able to publish a lot of work. However, the advice in this chapter hopes to nudge you toward purposeful efficiency, rather than encourage you to become a word-spurting machine. Some of the books mentioned in this chapter make for extremely useful reading, but to my mind they don't necessarily strike a balance between stunning short-term productivity and holistic long-term well-being. Nonetheless, when taken with a side order of the material in Chapter 8 (Nurture Your Creativity), there is much to be learned from authors who write thousands of words each day, or publish four books a year.

This chapter contains several ideas for pepping up your productivity, but you'll find some resonate with you more than others. Be sure to experiment, notice how your sense of ease changes, then choose what works for you.

What's Your Reasonable Writing Rate?

Knowing how many words you write in a typical session can be helpful both in planning your writing projects and in assessing whether your daily productivity is "good enough" for you personally.

The first time I bothered to assess how fast I write was when I took part in National Novel Writing Month. NaNoWriMo has a target of 50,000 words in the 30 days which make up November. That's roughly 1667 words per day, and I found I needed about two hours to write that many draft quality words. Notice I said *draft*: this was not award-winning fiction and frankly, not a quality I would want anyone else to read. But they were words on the page. Easing that pace a little tells me that I can probably manage about 700 first draft words per hour on a consistent basis, allowing for a more measured effort than the frantic, glorious sprint which characterizes NaNoWriMo.

Another structured novel writing program, the 85K Writing Challenge, allows you 90 days to draft 85,000 words, or about 950 a day, every January through March. That's a pace which allows room for the rest of your life, over a sustained period.

It doesn't matter if your hourly rate is faster or slower than these benchmarks, but I strongly suggest you work it out. If you don't want to take part in a hectic month-long challenge like NaNoWriMo, try three separate writing sessions and record your hourly output. Don't pick the most productive day: the one in the middle is probably more representative.

Author Sue Johnson, who has published in several genres, believes establishing a work pattern is important. "Put in regular amounts of work. Baby steps are fine—just keep going."

Want To Increase Your Pace a Little?

Before you get too concerned about your writing rate, know that dozens of famous writers worked at what they considered a lamentably slow pace. For every prolific writer like Anthony Trollope or P.G. Wodehouse, there were those who plodded. W.B. Yeats claimed he never penned more than five or six good lines in a day, while Gustave Flaubert was dismayed that *Madame Bovary* was progressing, at one point, at the rate of two pages in a week.

Nonetheless, if your output troubles you, it's perfectly possible to coax the words into coming a little faster. A wonderful book on this subject is Rachel Aaron's *2k to 10k*, which explains how to measure your current pace and then improve it using her triad of "Knowledge, Time, and Enthusiasm."

In addition, I strongly recommend embarking on NaNoWriMo at least once in your writing career. Regardless of whether or not you finish your 50,000 words, you'll practice the vital skill of writing your first draft fast, while minimizing doubt, backtracking, and self-editing. Or, as they call it, to write with literary abandon. For most people, who are unable to retreat to a cave for a whole month, this is simply the only way they come anywhere near progressing at the necessary rate to finish. The NaNoWriMo website has lots of resources on banishing your inner editor, while founder Chris Baty's book *No Plot? No Problem!* is an excellent, comforting guide to lighting a fire under your writing speed.

Set Goals

Now you know your hourly rate, I strongly encourage you to set some goals. The more specific you can be, the better.

Sue Johnson recommends you "Have an idea of what you would like to achieve in the next year with your writing. Create a 'success collage.' Find pictures and words in magazines. Pin this where you can see it. Spend a few minutes every day visualizing the achievement of a goal. Use all the senses!"

How do you know what an achievable goal would be for you? Take a look at your typical week and estimate accordingly. For example, if I'm aiming for a manuscript of about 70,000 words, I can likely draft that in about 100 hours. If I look at my typical week and know I can spend nine hours writing, that gives me an expectation that I should expect to complete a first draft in 11 or 12 weeks, allowing for a bit of contingency. This method gives you not only a deadline, but a breakdown of how many sessions and how many words per session will make that happen.

Now put those writing sessions on your calendar and prioritize them like any other appointment. To make your deadline feel even more real, Sue Johnson says, "Set a date for completion and plan a celebration."

If this forecasting approach doesn't alarm you, you might even enjoy looking at the comprehensive picture of your writing aspirations and rolling your sleeves up for some serious long-term planning. Many creative personalities resist a structure like this, but Elizabeth Ducie, whose published books include nonfiction, short stories, and thrillers, was a project planner in a former life. She advocates juggling multiple projects by "developing a list of objectives on an annual and a monthly basis and then preparing a detailed project plan for each objective. I use spreadsheets both for the lists and for the plans. The annual list just has items and due date; the plans are in the form of bar charts. Each month, I consult the bar chart and use it to construct my monthly plan. On a daily basis, I write a short To Do in my desk diary and tick each item off as it's done."

Whether your goals consist of a high level plan to write your next book, or a detailed system like Ducie's, let's now look at some further tactics to make sure words actually get onto paper, or your screen.

Just Start!

There's only so much pencil sharpening and keyboard dusting you can do before you face the inevitable: to write a book, you're going to have to write. So, get off Instagram, let the cat out, and just dive in. If even those three simple words cause your stomach to churn, the following three principles might give you the nudge you need to begin.

Getting Started Is the Hardest Part of Anything

I'm a runner, and on many days, the first 100 yards are the least appealing. Sometimes, I make a deal with myself that I just have to change into my running gear, leave the house, and jog to the end of the road. That, usually, is enough for me to keep going. There's also a technique called the five-minute rule, where you make an agreement with yourself that you'll do the dreaded task for just 300 seconds. Then, if you want to, you can stop without guilt. Somewhere around four minutes, magic often happens, and you find you're happy to keep going.

It Is *Never* the Right Time

Please don't wait for perfect conditions to start your book, lose five pounds, declutter your closet, or embark on any other valuable goal.

Actor and author Hugh Laurie provided some of my favorite wisdom on this. He said, "It is a terrible thing, I think, in life to wait until you are ready... There is almost no such thing as ready."

There is never a perfect time, you'll never feel entirely prepared, and conditions will never be ideal. If you're lucky, you'll have about 29,000 days on this earth. Don't waste another.

Women Think They Need a Qualification

In her book, *Playing Big*, Tara Mohr cautions that women, in particular, are likely to make excuses and effectively put a dream on hold because they don't feel academically qualified to pursue it. You might think you can't help others without a coaching certificate, you can't design websites without a Bachelor's degree, and you can't pen a novel without an MFA. None of these beliefs are true, and the inner voice telling you that is just trying to hold you back in a misguided attempt to avoid risk. Of course, I'm not advocating brain surgery without training. Just know you *don't* need to take a class or gain a certificate before you can write your book.

I must mention here that I did, in fact, complete a worthwhile online course with Media Bistro while drafting my first novel. The feedback offered me early reassurance that my work was good, and I took pleasure in finishing the curriculum as others dropped out. However, I don't think it made a significant impact on the quality of my writing.

So, by all means, take a class if you find it motivating and you form an inspiring connection with your teacher and other students. But never use lack of credentials as a reason not to write.

Habits and Rituals

By necessity, you'll need to switch gear fast from the other roles in your life to that of author. Rituals can help here, but use them mindfully. I went through a phase when I couldn't settle to write without a snack to munch on: that combination of butt-in-chair and chips-in-mouth really wasn't sustainable.

On the other hand, if you have a special chair, playlist, sweater, scented candle, or tea, to signal to your subconscious that you're now in writing mode, that might be very helpful. Experiment with each of your senses and find a healthy ritual which supports your inner scribe.

Habits to help you write and stay focused are a topic which Mason Currey explores at length in his book *Daily Rituals: How Artists Work*. Currey investigates the customary routines of over 150 creative luminaries, and although coffee does seem to feature strongly for many of them, he concludes that impeccable productivity is neither necessary, nor the norm. Most of the people he examined are, he says, "committed to daily work but never entirely confident of their progress. All of them made the time to get their work done. But there is infinite variation in how they structured their lives to do so."

Don't worry about behaviors which work for other authors but don't help you. History has been full of eccentric writers, many with unique habits. Thriller writer Patricia Highsmith, for example, loved snails and is said to have once attended a cocktail party with a hundred of them in her handbag. Friedrich Schiller, on the other hand, liked the smell of rotting apples, so kept a drawerful in the room where he worked. Not many of us would aspire to emulate these two.

In Chapter 1, did you identify where you write best? Turn this into a ritual if working at a café, laundromat, or in a train carriage helps you. But if this popular scribing tactic doesn't work for you, don't slavishly follow the wisdom of the crowd.

You'll find a printable writing tracker in the bonus downloads—use this to record if any rituals in particular work for you.

Small pleasures are important, too. Sue Johnson suggests, "Give yourself at least one treat per day—this doesn't have to be anything expensive!"

Busy Versus Productive

As an indie author you can spend hours on "busy" work which feels important but doesn't actually move the needle toward your goals. Social media is a prime example: checking, sharing, tweeting, following, commenting, pinning, liking, and posting can take hours every day. I'm a big believer in finding your indie tribe and supporting them (see Chapter 7), but you *must* set a time limit for this kind of activity. Also, restrict it to certain times of day—ideally, when you're tired and less productive, or have a ten-minute gap to fill—not when your energy is highest and/or you have a 40-minute undisturbed block of time for writing. Otherwise you're simply procrastinating, and stealing from your future success.

Of course, it's not just social media or surfing the web which can drag you away from the task at hand. Often, we interrupt ourselves with non-writing tasks which "suddenly" take on supreme importance. Do you sit down to a first draft but feel compelled to plan the week's meals instead? Did you intend to work on edits but find yourself cleaning out your sock drawer? Notice when you do this, and ask what's really going on.

Flattering invitations are also a form of interruption, but a big one. I've given talks which took me hours to plan and deliver, and attended book fairs which demolished an entire writing day, resulting in barely enough book sales to cover the cost of putting fuel in my car. In fairness, I've also been the guest of small, inauspicious groups and sold stacks of books. Make sure you pay attention to the characteristics of a successful event and be liberal with saying no graciously.

In fact, when asked for anything, whether it's your time or free books, try the default response of, "Let me have 24 hours to think about it." It buys you the all-important space you need to consider and, if necessary, decline. For more on saying no, you might enjoy the chapter on that topic in *The Year of Yes* by acclaimed TV writer Shonda Rhimes.

The skill of paying attention is key to nudge your time from simply being *busy* to actually being *productive* toward your goals. I know from personal experience how easy it is to get sucked into tempting activities. Practice asking yourself: "When I sat down at my computer, was this what I intended to do?" or, "If I devote half a day to that, will it help me reach my goals?" Every time you realize you've strayed, just come back gently to your main task. In time, you'll drift off less, and come back faster.

In his book *Die Empty*, Todd Henry defines what he calls shadow pursuits, as "activities that capture our attention and give us a sense of accomplishment, but serve as a substitute for the real work we know we should be doing." Your shadow pursuits might be small activities, like those above, or even entire, large projects which prevent you from working on your true calling. Keep a close eye on how you spend your time, and be prepared, on occasion, to ask yourself some tough questions.

Hold Yourself Accountable

Women's fiction author Heather Wardell sums up what many writers feel: "Focus is a huge challenge. There's always something else to do instead of writing, and often that 'something else' is easier or more immediately satisfying." Author Tracey Gemmell confirms the struggle: "There are as many, if not more, distractions in your solitary writing den as in any corporate office. It's easy to drift. Focus. Establish a routine. Set deadlines. Hold yourself accountable."

Check back on your personality type according to the Gretchen Rubin's Four Tendencies (see Chapter 1). This is key information as you attempt to stick to your stated goals. An Upholder, for example, can probably just knuckle down through their own willpower. But Obligers have a substantial need for a buddy or accountability partner, if they're to stay on track.

Experiment with reviewing your progress either daily or weekly. Many writers enjoy pinning a chart on the wall and awarding themselves daily colored stars for words achieved. During my weekly planning session, I'm careful to note my accomplishments as well as carrying forward the inevitable things which didn't get completed. These methods let you see if your goals are realistic, and whether it was a flawed goal or sloppy execution which undermined the outcome. Sue Johnson reminds us to "feel proud of what you've achieved," and recommends that, having completed a small step toward your goal, "Reward yourself for each one."

On an hour by hour level, you need to check in with yourself and confirm you are indeed working on what you intended. It's vital you remain mindful and that you stay vigilant about getting "sucked in" either to small distractions (for example, checking Facebook), or bigger projects, like learning a new social media platform, when that's not in your strategic plan. At first, you might find it helpful to set a gentle alarm for 20-minute intervals, to serve as your signal to ask "Is this what I ought to be doing?" I'm also a fan of an old-fashioned sand timer, which you invert to allow the grains to trickle through. You can buy these in various sizes; mine lasts an hour. There's something about that falling sand which reminds me every moment is a gift.

In terms of vigilance about whether you're working on what you resolved to work on, I can't say enough good things about meditation as a way of sharpening your ability to notice when your mind has strayed. Chapter 8 includes extensive tips on meditation, and I hope you'll enjoy the difference it makes.

Later, in Chapter 14, we'll look at identifying things you should decide not to worry about. I recommend keeping that list handy, to resist anxieties which do nothing but undermine your productivity.

The Myth of Writer's Block

My belief is that writer's block does not exist: all it means is you are failing to write sufficient words of a high enough quality to satisfy your standards.

Skeptical? OK, pick up a pencil. Can you write your name? Can you write a sentence about a dog walking down a road? No? Then try: "The dog walked down the road." You *can* still write, you're just not writing in the way you'd *hoped*.

Some days, words will tumble onto the page easily, and when you reread them, they might even be half decent. Other days, your prose will come more slowly and need significant CPR at the editing stage. You should absolutely expect your productivity to ebb and flow, and in fact I'd suggest you welcome it. Like nature's seasons, where spring and summer are full of vitality, followed by autumn and winter for rest and rejuvenation, your creativity and enthusiasm won't be constant. Don't put yourself under the pressure of expecting uniform output. I'd even go so far as to suggest it would be arrogant to see yourself as a non-stop writing machine.

So, when less productive times arrive, don't panic. Know that these lulls are normal. Give yourself permission to write a little less, or (at the draft stage) produce a quality you don't applaud. At these times, pay extra attention to investing in rest and creative rejuvenation. Heed the signal that your brain and soul need to regroup.

This doesn't mean you'll stop writing entirely, just that you demand less of yourself. You don't have writer's block, you're just trickling out words which will need further attention later. In her book *2k to 10k*, Rachel Aaron points out this approach actually protects, rather than diminishes, your overall writing pace: "If your goal is to become a faster writer, the single most efficient change you can make isn't actually upping your daily word count, but eliminating the days when you are not writing."

I already extolled the benefits of taking part in National Novel Writing Month, and training yourself to write and write and *write*, regardless of quality, is well worth the time commitment. As a NaNoWriMo participant, you learn quickly that in order to hit the challenging word count targets, you don't judge your first draft, you don't get depressed, you don't fall into despair, and you don't stop. Everything can be fixed later, and as author Jodi Picoult famously said, "You can't edit a blank page."

Take the words *writer's block* out of your vocabulary and your enjoyment as an indie author is guaranteed to take an upward leap.

Summary

Being an indie author means nobody else will hold your feet to the fire if the work isn't getting done, or, as Pamela Olivia Brown says, "Taking a book from concept to publication depends on *you*."

There are all kinds of techniques and tricks you can use to plan your writing time and make sure that words actually flow. I encourage you to calculate your typical writing rate and take steps to nudge it higher if that feels appropriate. Remember that getting started is the steepest part of the slope, and that habits can be enormously helpful. Find an accountability method which works for you, and hold yourself to your goals. But also recognize when your productivity is good enough, and when you tip into unreasonable self-criticism of your progress.

Self-Reflection Questions

1) What's your reasonable writing pace? Allowing for contingencies, how long, at this pace, will it take you to complete a draft? What small rewards will you give yourself along the way?

2) What are your current writing habits and rituals? Could you add any regular behaviors to your writing routine which would be helpful?

3) What tasks do you regularly engage in which might count as "busy" work, rather than moving you toward your goals? Note one of them and pin it where you work; see if you can catch yourself more often when you slip into this.

Chapter 6: Hone Your Craft

Before you get too deep into your author ambitions, get some honest feedback on your writing skills. This process isn't intended to dissuade or depress you, but serves instead as a pointer to areas where you most need to improve.

Make sure the input you receive balances improvement points with things you're doing well. The best feedback gives you a clear idea of strengths, which you can then build on, as well as weaknesses to address. Your creative ego is probably fragile and humans generally exhibit what's known as negativity bias, whereby we pay more attention to criticism than praise and dwell on negative news.

Options for receiving feedback include:
- Paying an editor for a short critique.
- Entering short story contests where feedback is provided.
- Finding an honest but kind friend. Ideally, they'd be a published author, but anyone who reads with a careful eye, and can explain the reasons behind their likes and dislikes, would be worthwhile.
- Asking your writing tribe (see Chapter 7). Naturally, you can return this favor.
- Posting a sample of your work on a platform such as Wattpad.

Take a deep, honest breath after this feedback, and decide on the split of time you need between improving your writing skills and working toward publication.

In addition, regardless of your current level, I recommend the following craft-building activities.

Read a Few Writing Books

Notice I said *a few*, not *endless* tomes on how to write. If in doubt, pick one each on plot, character, language, and something more general, for inspiration. You'll probably have too many to choose from, not too few, but if you're stuck, try:
- *The Plot Whisperer*, Martha Alderson
- *The Art of Character*, David Corbett
- *Vex, Hex, Smash, Smooch*, Constance Hale
- *Bird by Bird*, Anne Lamott

Lamott's advice is particularly cherished by the writing community. Tracey Gemmell confirms, "If you only read one book on writing, read Anne Lamott's *Bird by Bird*. It gave me permission to fail, to get up again, to move on and to succeed in my goals. I give it credit for me still being here three years into my writing career."

In case it's not obvious, the reason I don't suggest you read dozens of writing books is that you're a writer, and writers *write*. After all, you can't become a figure skater by reading about it. Also, if you're not careful, too much reading (by those who are, or appear to be, phenomenally successful in their efforts) will allow self-doubt to breed within you. You'll want to learn and improve through your whole writing career, so reading books on the craft can be an ongoing supplement to your own work, not an enormous hurdle before you even start.

Read Books by Other Authors

There is rich learning to be gained by consuming as many books as possible by other authors. I'd suggest spending about half your reading time within your genre, and half outside.

Within your genre, try to find good indie authors and not-so-good, as well as traditionally published bestsellers. Develop your reading eye so you notice what the author has done well, and what you might change:
- Which "rules" did they break, and did their gamble succeed?
- Which words or concepts, if any, were overused?
- What did you make of the cover design? What would you change about it?
- For fiction, how was the plot pacing? Did the blurb represent the story you read?
- For nonfiction, did the book deliver the information or transformation it promised? Was the structure logical?

Reading outside your genre is wonderful for creativity, and you might find spotting the elements listed above a little easier when you're not immersed in your favorite type of book.

If you enjoy a book by another author, be sure to review it online and let them know, too. Your current reading, and books you'd recommend, also make great fodder for your author newsletter.

Join a Writing Group

If you're joining or starting a writing group, please be cautious and stay mindful about whether it really works for you. It can be incredibly hard to find a local group which truly meets your needs, so do consider online groups too. Fiction author Wendy Janes found the ideal group for her was on Facebook: "I'll always be grateful for the wonderful support I received from the Chick Lit Goddesses when I first started writing (and I don't even write Chick Lit)."

Don't forget, a writing group can be a group of two, if a single accountability partner works better for you.

You might need some tenacity and patience before you discover, or create, the writing group you need. Pitfalls of groups include:
- People who are not at the same stage of their writing career as you. For example, if you've published two novels but they haven't finished a draft chapter, you may feel stymied.
- People who want different things from the writing and publishing process. Some groups exist purely for writing critique, while other authors support each other with business-related activities too.
- Those who never actually move forward in their publishing journey. If you're intent on publishing but others are content to edit indefinitely, that can lead you to question the readiness of your work.
- Those who only attend so they can hear their own voice reading their own words.
- Those who give vague, misjudged, overcritical, or downright malicious feedback.

Your creative spark might, of course, benefit greatly from these interactions, but don't hesitate to get your writing support somewhere else, if these sessions don't energize, inspire or inform you. Tracey Gemmell warns, "Trust your voice. Writing by committee... is the deathtrap of the rookie author. Keep the 'i' in 'mine.'"

Read Agent Blogs

Even if you have no intention of submitting your work to a literary agent, it doesn't hurt to read a few articles about what they're looking for and what turns them off. If an agent would stop reading on the first page of your book, there's a fair chance your readers will too.

However, always take this information in the context that agents have *extremely* specific wishlists and they're usually in business to acquire books which will sell in colossal numbers. One of the joys of being indie is you can write for a niche market, or produce a book which is personally important to you, or succeed in a genre where traditional publishing finds margins too tight. For example, industry hearsay now suggests that ebook prices in romance are too low for traditional publishers (with their weighty cost structures) to be able to make reasonable profits.

Don't forget, though, there are as many opinions about what makes a publishable book as there are readers. I encountered a memorable agent blog which practically forbade starting your novel with the main character waking up in the morning. Soon after, I found myself on page one of international bestseller *Gone Girl*. In other words, always take comfort that rules are made to be broken.

Watch Webinars

Webinars are a phenomenal resource. Successful, savvy, innovative writers regularly gather online to share tips, insights, and techniques. You don't have to travel to attend, and chances are, the session is free. One of my favorites is the Self-Publishing Advice Conference, hosted twice a year by the Alliance of Independent Authors (ALLi).

The downside is that webinars can still be time-consuming, you can be blinded by interesting ideas and lose focus of what your core work is (see Chapter 5), and there is an "opportunity cost" that the time you invest is time lost from not writing your own book.

Here are my strict guidelines I use when watching a webinar:
- Keep in mind the person presenting almost always has something to sell. This is tools-for-gold-miners territory (see Chapter 13 for my soapbox sermon on that subject), so remember the webinar speaker is unlikely to be truly impartial.

- If you don't get at least one new, actionable tip in the first 15 minutes, leave.
- Avoid depressing yourself through comparisons. The presenter may have worked 50 hours a week for five years on their writing business. They may measure "sales" in a creative way. They can only sell their product or service to you if they convince you they are (way) more successful than you. So don't beat yourself up if their results appear far better than yours: you have your own constraints and your own publishing hopes. See Chapter 15 for further cautions about comparisons.

Elizabeth Lovick suggests that you look for a webinar or class you *need*, instead of one that's already in your comfort zone: "If you can find classes on the business side of indie publishing, go to those. If you are used to writing you won't need help with that part, but the business side is (dare I say it?) even more important."

Attend a Writing Conference

Surely few things are as heady, inspirational, and downright overwhelming as attending a conference specifically for writers. It's likely to be a huge investment of your money as well as time, so do approach this idea wisely.

Unless neither the clock nor your cash flow cause you much concern, I'd suggest you don't put a conference on your calendar until you have at least completed a first draft of your first book. If you haven't yet written that much, there's a risk the conference is a sophisticated form of procrastination. Prove to yourself you've got what it takes to be an author: finish that darn draft first!

On the other hand, if you can attend by volunteering and travel costs are low, the inspiration you stand to derive would be worthwhile at any stage of your writing career.

How to Choose a Writing Conference

- Location and cost will of course be important factors, but don't base your choice on these alone.
- Read blog posts by people who attended in previous years: get a sense of whom the conference is truly aimed at. Did they get out of it what you hope to?
- Get hold of the conference agenda from a previous year (if this year is not yet published). If the sessions don't excite you and don't feel relevant, give it a miss.
- As an indie author, watch for signs that the conference is friendly or unfriendly to you. If the key selling points are ability to connect with agents, and if there is no self-publishing track, know that you may feel like a second class citizen. Of course, you can still attend to work on your craft, and many of the marketing sessions will be relevant too. Just be wary of the subtle messages you might absorb about your chosen path.

How to Get the Most Out of a Conference

Are you an introvert? If so, brace yourself: a conference might drain you more than you realize. Even if you're an extrovert, don't be so busy making new friends that you don't turn your learning into action. Here are my top tips:

- Stay at the conference hotel, if you can. Days are likely to be long and jam-packed, so convenience is key. This will also mean you can retreat to your room for a quick time-out, if you need it. You'll probably need to book early to secure a room at a reasonable rate.
- Ahead of time, identify two or three key goals for attending. Knowing what you'd most like to get out of the experience will help you focus and not be overwhelmed by all that's on offer.

- If there are people with whom you'd especially like to connect, research them in advance. You can make (brief) contact on social media to let them know you're looking forward to their session. There's no harm being prepared with a couple of conversation openers, so that if you do find yourself in the elevator with a keynote speaker, you won't be tongue-tied. If in doubt, ask something like, "How was your morning?" and go from there.
- If possible, read a book by the keynote speaker in advance. You'll get more out of their talk as a result.
- Research the schedule before you arrive: if there are parallel sessions and you're torn between topics, visit the speakers' websites to get a sense of their perspective and likely material.
- Bring business cards (people really do forget these!), highlighter pens, and cheap pens to lend. Snacks might be wise, too.
- Pace yourself for energy. Skip sessions if you need to. Many writers are introverts and everyone's energy is likely to dip by the last day. But remember it costs nothing to smile.
- During or just after sessions, I like to use those highlighter pens to mark my notes with "to-do" items and "a-ha" insights.
- You'll probably be exhausted after the conference and dive directly back into your everyday life and/or day job. It's essential to block off further time in your calendar (aim for three or four weeks after) to review your notes and distill actions.
- Don't forget to follow up with anyone you met who was helpful, or with whom you'd simply like to stay in touch. You'd be surprised how few people take the trouble to do this. For other novice writers, ask them how you can best help their writing career.

Attendee Etiquette

Writing conferences draw a broad spectrum of people. If you are business minded and action oriented, you may find yourself frustrated by some common etiquette slips.

- Don't be the person who starts a question with a long explanation of their own circumstances. If your query needs that context to make sense, it's not a question, it's a request for a free consultation. If the speaker's answer doesn't benefit other attendees too, you've been selfish.
- Be ready to describe your book, or Work In Progress, in ten words or less. When you chat with someone in the queue for lunch, they *do not* want to hear a synopsis. And don't assume they're intimately familiar with your genre. There's no harm in referencing really famous books to help orient other writers. Saying "Harry Potter with recipes for kids" or "*Gone With the Wind* but set in space in 2081" would be neat, intriguing ways to summarize.
- Before you attend a session, research any words in the description you don't understand. If the title is "Six KDP reports you must use," don't be the laggard who asks for an explanation of what KDP is. It's a courtesy to speakers and other attendees to educate yourself on the *absolute basics* of a topic first.

Summary

Hopefully as an indie author you're committed to bringing your readers your best work, and developing and improving your skills as your writing experience deepens. You have a complete spectrum of options open to you, including reading, webinars, and attending conferences. You can also work carefully with other writers if you find a group which is supportive and appropriate for your needs. Be sure to balance the time you spend investing in your craft with the time you allow for the actual task of writing. Don't forget: writers write!

Self-Reflection Questions

1) What are your current reading habits? What mix of books in your own genre and outside do you tend to read? Do you need to add any classic writing books to your mix, or have you consumed enough for now?

2) Have you explored options for joining a writing group, either in person or online? If you've tried a group, in which ways did it work well—and not so well—for you? If you haven't tried a group, what key things would you be looking to get out of it?

3) What webinars and conferences can you find which you'd be interested in attending, if not soon, then in the future? Start to gather a list of possible learning events which might match your time, budget, and needs.

Chapter 7: Build Your Tribe

Would you like to belong to a tribe of cheerleaders, quality boosters, mentors, and sage advisers? People who'll nudge you along and publicly declare themselves excited to read your next book? Other authors can be amazing advocates and building a support network is a rewarding use of your time.

What's in It for You?

Invest some effort now in building your writing tribe and before long you'll find you have a willing, trustworthy, qualified group of book lovers who might:
- Critique your Work In Progress.
- Connect you with subject matter experts. For example, do you need to ask a stem cell scientist some questions? Ask your tribe if they know someone in that field.
- Beta read, to provide valuable feedback for your nearly complete manuscript.
- Serve as advance reviewers.
- Boost your launch day efforts on social media.
- Give you promotional tips, including what hasn't worked for them.
- Collaborate with you in events, group promotions, and even box sets.
- Refer you to professional services they've used.
- Possibly even buy and review your book, without you asking.
- General moral support and camaraderie (see Chapter 15).

Martha Reynolds found a local group of nearly 300 authors, which she loves. "One of the best things I ever did was join ARIA (The Association of Rhode Island Authors). Lots of marketing opportunities, terrific networking, and the annual Book Expo in December give me a chance to sell books locally. Previously, I belonged to a smaller group that focused more on writing. I didn't need that, though—I needed to sell books! ARIA showcases dozens of opportunities throughout the year for authors—farmers' markets, festivals, arts fairs, etc."

By contrast, Elizabeth Lovick, who lives in Orkney, Scotland, didn't let the remoteness of her home stop her finding her tribe: "I would say that writing and publishing indie nonfiction is a very lonely journey. Whilst the net is brilliant, and makes research for both the subject and the business options easier, it also means you can work away for months without seeing another person in the same boat as you are. Friends may be helpful, but usually they just say 'that's nice, dear'! Online industry friends can be very useful here—they will be going through the same thing."

Start Forming Connections

Don't be starstruck when it comes to forming connections with other authors. Simply reach out and you might be surprised at the friendliness of the response. Indie authors, in particular, are likely to welcome knowing you.

Find like-minded writers and authors by:
- Joining an online or offline group.
- Attending conferences or local writing events.
- Reaching out by email or on social media, to let someone know you enjoyed their work.
- Reading blogs by similar writers and commenting on the posts.

How You Can Help Others in the Writing Community

Not surprisingly, the list is similar to the things that other writers might also do for you:
- Offer to beta read.
- Read and review their new releases. When you read for pleasure, it's essential you leave constructive, honest online reviews. (However, never get into a situation where you're simply *trading* positive reviews with other authors. This isn't ethical and, ultimately, is a disservice to readers.)
- Carefully and kindly let them know—privately—if you spot any terrible errors in their published work.
- Feature their books on publication day, on your social media and/or blog. Visit a couple of places on their online book tour and leave an upbeat comment.
- Mention their work on social media at other times. For authenticity, stick to praising books you've read and truly enjoyed.
- Give away their books (you can gift an ebook) to your newsletter subscribers from time to time. This is a nice "filler" when you don't have big book news of your own, and is inexpensive.
- Ask your library to obtain a copy of their book(s).
- Show up for readings or book launch parties in your local area.
- Volunteer to help co-ordinate an event like NaNoWriMo, or with a local literacy program.
- Recommend another author for an opportunity which isn't quite right for you.
- Make books your go-to gift for birthdays and other occasions. Ideally, you might choose to support indie authors, but *any* book purchase earns you karma points. Tracey Gemmell feels especially strongly about this: "If you're only reading the 99c or free

download books, you can't expect readers to pay more for your work. Support other authors."
- Offer simple encouragement. You never know when someone is close to the end of their writing rope. A few kind words from you could make the difference between writing their next book... or giving up entirely.

Summary

As a committed indie author, you likely understand the concept that a rising tide lifts all ships. And I've no doubt that you enjoy a good book, otherwise you're in the wrong business. So it makes sense that boosting awareness of other authors is a collegial, karma-enhancing thing to do.

What's more, if you invest a little time and build goodwill, you can receive almost priceless returns. Other authors will be a positive influence on the quality of your own work, save you from expensive mistakes, and lend a hand to your promotional efforts. There's a comforting ease from knowing others have got your back.

Self-Reflection Questions

1) Identify an author whose work you've recently enjoyed, who is not yet a household name. How could you reach out?

2) Google "indie author" plus your genre, and see which new writers you discover. What can you learn from their online presence?

3) Track down the last five books you've enjoyed. Did you leave online reviews for these? Make this a habit, whenever you finish a book.

4) What help would you most like to receive from other authors? And how are you presently best placed to help them?

Chapter 8: Nurture Your Creativity

Your creative flair is your biggest single asset as an author. Just as a ballet dancer takes extreme care of his or her legs and feet, you must protect, nourish, and refresh your creativity. And since your overall well-being is the foundation of your innovation, this chapter also implores you to prioritize self-care.

Capture Your Ideas

Allow your muse to lead you where it will, but for goodness' sake capture those ideas, whenever they strike. You can carry a notebook, phone, index cards, or (temporarily) scribble on the back of your hand. You might even want all of these at your disposal, as long as you're disciplined at gathering your scattered ideas on a regular basis. In her iconic writing memoir, *Bird by Bird*, Anne Lamott paints a wonderful picture of this habit: "I took notes on the people around me, in my town, in my family, in my memory... I learned to be like a ship's rat, veined ears trembling, and I learned to scribble it all down."

Unless you can't bear working digitally, it's preferable to store your ideas in a format you can backup, such as a Google doc or Evernote, and decide on categories according to your genre. You can see my organizing structure in Chapter 4.

It's likely you'll have far more ideas than you can work on at one time. That's normal for creative people and you can lessen the risk of indecisive overload by capturing them safely. This gives you the comfort of knowing they'll be there, when you're ready to return to them.

Boost Your Creativity

What if you do, temporarily, find yourself a little short of ideas? Or your writing feels homogeneous and predictable? My favored ways to boost your creativity include:
- Travel, even just a few miles. A change of scene will prompt new challenges for your characters.
- People watch. Hang around the lobby of a large hotel, go to a trade show, or find a café window on a busy street. Challenge yourself to create short vignettes about the strangers you see. Why is that man so anguished? Why is that couple peering under their car? Does he have allergies, or is he crying? What did she just steal, and why? If his pay check is late, what consequences does that have?
- Browse random magazines in a good bookstore, especially titles you would never usually pick up.
- Read the news. I particularly love the smaller, bizarre articles. The strangest things really *do* happen.
- Try a tangential hobby. Even if writing is your main form of artistic expression, you'll boost your originality by sketching, singing, dancing, sewing, coloring, or dabbling in any number of creative activities. Resist any internal pressure to produce something of acceptable quality: view this as pure fun and enjoy the process, not the results.
- Watch a movie you love. Identify the major plot points. How are characters revealed? Are there any scenes which don't move things forward? What happens at the halfway mark?
- Open a dictionary and pick a word with your eyes closed. Write a funny sentence which incorporates that word. Do it again, but this time make your sentence scary.

Self-Care

The quick creativity boosts mentioned above are helpful on a day-to-day basis, but don't expect to make endless "withdrawals" from your creative reserves without replenishing them too. Otherwise, you jeopardize not only your productivity, but your joy in the process too.

Some people characterize writing as a marathon, not a sprint. I think they're wrong: a long-term indie author career is more like running a marathon in every US state. Certainly, after the first few races you might find your technique improves, but it's a commitment which takes endurance, tenacity, and vigilant self-care.

Self-help and motivational author Grace Allison Blair knows that when creativity stalls, it "means I must take time to take care of myself, first. Often I will meditate and pray to receive inner knowledge to boost my inner gifts."

Breaks

Even if you find yourself with all day to write (and you probably won't), taking frequent breaks is vital for both your mind and body. On an hour by hour basis, the famous Pomodoro technique gives mini breaks after head down work periods. Personally, I tend to use the "laundry method" (should I trademark that?) where a load of washing takes roughly the length of my attention span. During the editing stages, Wendy Janes simply sets a timer for a specific duration. "When that alarm goes off," she says, "it's time to stop." Furthermore, "When you realize you've spent the last 20 minutes on the same sentence swapping a comma for a semicolon half a dozen times, you're unlikely to be using your time productively, let alone creatively."

There's nothing new about the concept of quiet time. Anyone with a passing knowledge of the Bible is aware of the distinction made for one-seventh of the week. But, if you need further convincing of the value of breaks and how famous figures in history have used them, take a look at the examples of productivity in Alex Soojung-Kim Pong's *Rest: Why You Get More Done When You Work Less*.

And it's worth remembering this truism: the days when you think you can't afford to take a break are the days you need one most.

Exercise and Fresh Air

I've mentioned already that I'm a runner: the slow, dogged but determined kind. I use it to de-stress, reset, and to unravel plot problems. You may not want to run marathons (in fact, I recommend you don't—the training gobbles up writing time at a worrisome rate!), but every writer should treat themselves to regular movement and ideally fresh air. Both your body and your brain will thank you; your chi and your chapters will end up better for it.

Grace Allison Blair has noticed the benefits of this approach: "Taking a walk can move my energy to receive a picture or small nuance from the inner knowing that will propel me into the next part of the story."

This notion was backed up by a 2014 Stanford University study by Marily Oppezzo and Daniel L. Schwartz, who showed in four separate experiments that "walking boosts creative ideation in real time and shortly after." They concluded, "Walking opens up the free flow of ideas, and it is a simple and robust solution to the goals of increasing creativity and increasing physical activity."

So, if you think you're stuck (see Chapter 5 for the myth of writer's block), or you're experiencing doubt about the quality of your work or ability to finish, I wholeheartedly recommend a bracing walk to renew and reinvigorate. In fact, researchers George Mammen and Guy Faulkner at the University of Toronto reviewed 25 different research articles and confirmed that, in the long term, moderate exercise can prevent episodes of depression. So take hold of your writerly blues, and get up and move.

Sleep

I get hopping mad when I see advice to writers to "make" time by getting up an hour earlier to work on their book. This is a fine plan and one I'm happy to support, but only if you compensate by going to bed earlier. Wendy Janes suggests, "Turn off your phone/PC/tablet before midnight—every night."

The human brain is a delicate organ and sleep deprivation will not only kill your creativity but wreck your productivity, and eventually your health too. In her book *The Sleep Revolution*, Ariana Huffington makes a compelling case for the importance of sleep. Please don't put your life at risk for the sake of your manuscript.

That said, what if you're in bed for a healthy number of hours but struggle with insomnia? Maybe you can't fall asleep, or you get a few hours' shuteye and then wake, restless, in the wee small hours? I've suffered from this too, so here are some favorite techniques and insights:

- Count backwards from 300, in increments of three. So, you'd imagine the numbers 300, 297, 294, 291, 288, 285, and so on. This is challenging enough to keep your mind off other things, but repetitive enough that you'll likely drift off before you get to zero. Perfectionists must resist the temptation to check constantly whether you've made a mistake—even if you suspect your numbers are no longer divisible by three, that's irrelevant, just keep going.
- It's been said that if you fall asleep for less than ten minutes, you may not realize you nodded off. I couldn't find a scientific study to back that up, but the sleep community does recognize the state of hypnagogia, where you're between the states of sleeping and being awake, along with the rare condition of pseudoinsomnia, where people feel like they're lying anxiously awake, despite actually being asleep. In any case, I find it comforting to tell myself

I'm getting more rest than I realize. Try it, and you'll find it removes much of the anxiety of not sleeping.
- Parenthood, of course, robs you of sleep like little else. Historical fiction author Melissa Addey says, "Being sleep deprived is awful, but bear in mind that often our good ideas come to us when we teeter between sleep and waking. Keep a notebook handy—for moments of inspiration or just zombie-like ramblings."
- In fact, a notebook by the bed is a good idea, whether or not you're a parent. If an important task (or plot twist) darts into your brain at 3AM, jot it down. Then sleep a little more soundly, knowing it will be there for you in the morning. I love the suggestion that a pencil is less risky to use in the dark, as you'll avoid getting ink on your sheets.
- If sleep is truly elusive, get up, and try a light snack or comforting drink (such as hot milk, not alcohol!). Don't look at your phone or another screen—the blue light really could damage your chances of nodding off.
- Try an app which offers sleep sounds or a sleep story, which is a gentle audio tale designed to lull you back to dreamland. Given that I could never fall asleep to the drone of a cassette player when I was a child, I was astonished when this worked for me.
- Call on your daytime meditation practice (see below) to notice when your mind is racing, and gently bring it back.
- If all else fails, reassure yourself that just lying quietly in bed does restore your body somewhat. It may not be as ideal as sleep, but horizontal relaxation is still beneficial.

Retreats

A writing retreat doesn't have to be expensive, fancy, or led by a bestselling author. But once or twice a year, try to get away for two to three days to focus entirely on writing. Look back at Chapter 1 (How Do You Respond to Expectations?) to determine whether going away solo is likely to work for you, or if you'll need an accountability partner.

Retreat tips:
- To save money, book a local hotel at the last minute. Consider using a website reservation service which offers a great deal if you don't select the actual hotel. As long as you have a desk and power supply, you can write.
- You can also keep costs down by swapping homes with a friend. Be sure to resist the temptation to spring clean your place ahead of time: that will likely steal more writing time than you create.
- Get together with other writers if that will genuinely stimulate you, and not just turn into wine-in-the-hot-tub gossip sessions!
- Attend an organized writing retreat if you yearn for structure and/or literary coaching. The monetary investment will help you (and others in your life) see this as a serious priority.

Ergonomics and Eyesight

I'm no expert on ergonomics, but my advice is to pay close attention to how your body feels both when you write, and after. Experiment with different writing locations, using your mouse with your other hand, standing for periods of time, and dictation software. For an excellent introduction to speaking your book, I recommend Chapter 11 in *The Juggling Author* by Jim Heskett.

Never ignore physical niggles, even minor ones. Get help quickly and you might be surprised how pains can be mitigated. Last year I experienced sudden shoulder agony which, if unresolved, would have destroyed my joy in writing. I had the good fortune to show up (reluctantly) for an employer-sponsored personal training session; the fitness instructor took one look at my shoulder and ordered pressure exercises using a lacrosse ball and the nearest wall. Within two days, and with an investment of less than $5, almost all of my discomfort was gone.

I'm not saying you should treat all your writing agonies with a bright yellow ball and obviously I'm not qualified to give medical advice. But I'm the proof that simple remedies can work. Don't delay until you have a serious problem, seek help when it's just a twinge.

Likewise, your eyesight is a precious gift. Take breaks, and guard against eyestrain. The 20-20-20 exercise can be helpful here: every 20 minutes, take a 20-second break and focus your eyes on something at least 20 feet away.

Also, please don't ignore visual warning signs. If your sight is suffering, there are many options open to you, including the Bates Method which offers natural eyesight improvement based on relearning the habits of good sight. Bates Teacher Charlotte Schuman decided to give the method "a proper try" after her vision deteriorated to the point where she couldn't get by without glasses. She says, "I cannot emphasize enough how worthwhile the method is and how worthy it is of more credibility and acceptance worldwide."

Meditation

Chances are, you're either already practicing meditation or you think it's a total load of baloney. If you're in the second camp, please try this: stop thinking of it as meditation, and start thinking of it as *practicing paying attention*.

I'm convinced there are profound physiological benefits of meditation... but I'm not sure I've achieved any of them yet! However, what *has* been invaluable to me is developing the skill of noticing what I'm thinking. In today's ultra-wired world, with so much on our to-do lists, most of us suffer from monkey mind. As Dinty W. Moore describes in his book *The Mindful Writer*: "The brain is likely to go suddenly hyperactive, leaping from notion to notion, idea to idea, like a caffeine-fueled monkey swinging from tree to tree."

So, we're either trying to do four things at once, or we're dwelling on a mistake made yesterday, or we're planning a task for tomorrow. Given that "today is the tomorrow we worried about yesterday" (this quote is generally believed to be from Dale Carnegie), we're robbing ourselves of the joy of the task at hand. Many of our thoughts are downright unhelpful, berating for what's past, self-doubting about the present, or unnecessarily pessimistic about the future. We fall into absolute thinking (see Chapter 15), such as, "This always happens to me," or, "I should have known I'd never finish this book". Paying attention to your thoughts is a priceless skill. It's altered my life and I'm on a mission to spread the word. Picking up this knack could be the biggest transformation you'll ever make.

From my own experience, I believe meditation will bring you benefits in various ways:
- Minimize procrastination: you'll catch yourself getting sucked into low value activities you didn't truly intend to do.
- Increase focus: once you do settle to a task, your brain will stay with it more easily.
- Reduce stress: even if your thoughts still skip around, you'll notice that's happening and be able to remind yourself that getting mired in a worry, memory, or plan isn't helpful right now.
- Improve relationships: you'll do a better job of being present with people you care about, and you're more likely to rescue a conversation that's heading in a destructive direction. (I've caught myself on the brink of picking a fight with my husband, and I'm convinced my meditation practice has generated just enough awareness to choose another path.)

Mark Abramson, founder of Stanford University's Mindfulness-Based Stress Reduction Program, puts it like this: "The reward of meditation is that it enables us to begin taking back our ability to choose the direction of our lives—

which incorporates how we treat ourselves, our health and how we interact with others."

In other words, Abramson is acknowledging that it's not just our thoughts which are flitting off, doing their own thing. Our habits and daily choices desperately need some attention too. Why are you eating that (again)? Why are you slumped on the couch watching that TV show (again)? Why did you just hit the snooze button for the fourth time? Why did you just spend an hour on YouTube? Once developed, the skill of paying attention saves you from a spectrum of mindless actions.

If you've never tried meditation before, here are steps to get started:

1. Identify a ten-minute slot in your day. Ideally, this will be at the same time each day, and right after something you always do—such as brushing your teeth or drinking your first cup of coffee. When I worked in an office, I used to drive to work and park, then meditate before going into the building. Traffic uncertainty was out of the way, but I was not yet gripped by emails and workplace demands.
2. Set a timer. There is a meditation app, Calm (free and paid options available), which I really like, but any timer will do.
3. Sit somewhere quiet where you won't be disturbed. If you use public transit, headphones can create this safe space for you, but you'll need a little practice at tuning out jolts and service announcements. You don't need a fancy space and a floor cushion. I had great success in the driver's seat of my car. Try not to lie down: personal experience suggests you'll probably fall asleep, which is lovely, but not the point.
4. Close your eyes and take note of the seat beneath you, and your feet touching the floor. Wriggle a little to get comfortable and gently let go of a little tension in your jaw, neck, shoulders, and back.

5. Take a few deep breaths, filling your lungs completely and letting the air out in a big sigh.
6. Now allow your breathing to return to normal and simply try to focus on each in-breath and each out-breath.
7. Here's the magic: your mind *will* wander. That's okay, in fact that's perfect. (Expert meditators might not suffer from this much, but we mortals do, and it's ideal, it's why we're doing this.) Your job, and your only job, is to *notice* each time your thoughts stray, and *gently* invite your focus back to your breath.
8. That's it. Just notice and come back. Don't follow the thought, let it go. Don't judge yourself for having it. In fact, congratulate yourself for noticing.
9. When your timer goes off, take some further deep breaths, wriggle your fingers and toes, and gently open your eyes. An optional ending: with your eyes still closed, rub your palms together briskly, then cup them over your eyes to offer some gentle, natural heat. Open your eyes into the semi-darkness offered by your hands. This is a really nurturing way to finish.
10. Repeat the next day, and the next. Add an extra session if you're having a truly wretched day.

In time, you'll get better at noticing when your thoughts wander during your meditation. And here's the genius part: you'll start to notice at other times of day, too. Dinty W. Moore writes, "Through the simple awareness of breathing, you can eventually expand your mindfulness to the more complex and involuntary actions of your life."

If you try nothing else from this chapter, it's worth giving meditation a shot. Your productivity, relationships, and peace of mind all stand to benefit. Please ditch any weary assumptions you might have about meditating and add the *skill of paying attention* as something you plan to develop.

Self-compassion

We creative types can be harsh judges of ourselves. Even if we're not all going around cutting off an ear like Vincent Van Gogh, I bet there are times you've told yourself your work is worthless, unoriginal, or just plain blah.

So here's a two-part rule. Part one, practice paying attention (see above). I assured you it would have far-reaching benefits, and here's one. Part two, when you notice a thought, run it through the friend test. That means, would you say that aloud to a close friend, who was experiencing the same difficulty?

For example, would you say:
- "Bob, you're right, you'll never lose that weight. Give up now, you fat slob."
- "Carol, of course you don't stand a chance getting that promotion. I don't know why you ever put yourself forward, you conceited idiot."
- "Arjun, I don't know why you started that novel. You clearly won't ever finish it and in any case, it isn't any good."

You simply wouldn't say any of that to a good friend, and probably not to a frenemy, either. So, ease up, and don't say it to yourself. What would you say instead?
- "Bob, I know this is hard for you. How can I help you with your healthy eating habits?"
- "Carol, how could you feel better prepared for your interview? Remember, even if you don't get this promotion, there will be other chances."
- "Arjun, just keep writing and you will finish. I know you can do it. I believe in you."

Even author Jim Heskett, who boasts a publishing pace of four books a year and aspires to be "a perpetual motion fiction machine," recognizes the need to forgive yourself for setbacks and stumbles. In his book *The Juggling Author* he suggests, "Maybe you need to take your writing career one day at a time. Or one hour at a time. Being too harsh on yourself isn't going to do you any good."

One of the leading experts on self-compassion is Kristin Neff, and she offers online resources on her website, Self-Compassion.

Quick Energy Boosts

This chapter is full of ideas for protecting and increasing your long-term energy, but you'll also encounter moments when you need a quick pick-me-up. Writing is an arduous process and no matter how smartly you manage your time, there will be occasions when your energy simply slumps. Here are easy suggestions for some emergency zing:
- Go outside and breathe deeply.
- Play with an animal.
- Dance for five minutes.
- Do ten jumping jacks.
- Drink something chilled.
- Turn up the volume on music which lifts you.

Summary

Creativity is the secret sauce of writing effectively and enjoyably, so it's imperative you nurture and refresh this resource.

As Grace Allison Blair puts it, "If you take care of your body, and make friends with your mind and emotions, you can have the abundant creativity that will fuel your imagination for all your life."

The good news is that time you invest in self-care will benefit every area of your life, not just your scribing endeavors. There are dozens of ways to feed inspiration and foster well-being, so by being open to different options you can begin to develop tactics which suit your preferences and circumstances. But if you try just one new suggestion from this chapter, I'd be thrilled to hear it was meditation.

Self-Reflection Questions

1) How are you currently capturing your ideas? Do you need to add any new methods for ease and convenience?

2) Can you identify one or two new self-care habits to adopt? Find a printable self-care tracker in the bonus downloads.

Part 3: Finesse Your Process

Chapter 9: Balance Life With Writing

I strongly suspect you don't live alone in a mountain cabin, so that you can write every morning without fail. You don't then eat lunch, take a hike, meditate, bike to town for groceries, and spend the evening reading. Don't worry: none of us do. The reality for every author I know is that they have a life, responsibilities, and identity apart from their literary endeavors. This chapter has suggestions for managing that blend more gracefully.

Time Fragments Are Your Friends

If you ever want to complete your book, you simply can't wait for a free Saturday before working on it. That is the surest route to an unfinished manuscript. Instead, make your peace with seizing little chunks of time—fragments—which you must use productively. How?

- I'm not necessarily an advocate of writing *every* day. Instead, write often enough that you can remember what's going on in your book. That might be daily for you, or you might find every other day is fine. You need to be familiar enough with what you just wrote, so that you can get some further useful words on the page in just 15 minutes. Claire Cook, author of *Must Love Dogs* and many other novels, famously wrote in a minivan while waiting for her kids at their activities.
- Sort out your technology so you can write a first draft almost anywhere. This might mean your phone, a Google doc, or dictating your book with speech recognition software. Literature professor and novelist-in-progress Kim Manganelli carries a small Moleskine notebook with her and writes as

little as a few sentences at a time, typing them up later.
- See Chapter 5 for suggestions on how to remain focused, including my own preference, a sand timer.
- Take comfort from the Roman poet Lucretius: "The fall of dropping water wears away the stone."

Pat Edwards (who does believe in writing every day) goes so far as to calculate what those slivers of time mean to her: "I set a short time period (20 minutes) during lunch... If you think 20 minutes sounds too short to accomplish anything, just do the math. In a month, that's 400 minutes or 6.6 hours of writing. That's not counting any work you do on the weekends!"

Or, to take an example from my own life, when I began meditating for ten minutes a day, the app I use kept track of total time spent. Within a year—and without anything like a perfect daily habit—I'd invested 50 hours. What could you achieve in 50 hours? A great deal, I'm sure. If you manage 15 minutes of writing, six days a week, you'll be almost 80 hours further ahead than you would be if you waited for those mythical free Saturdays.

"Little and often" is far, far better than "lots but hardly ever."

Family Support and Boundaries

In Chapter 1 when you considered your true priorities, it's likely family members ranked high on your list of the most important things in your life. That's normal and appropriate, but it doesn't mean you have to prioritize them at every single moment. In fact, you'll need to set some clear expectations to prevent your dearest destroying your writing time.

If you have a partner, hopefully they support your writing goals. If not, change the conversation, change your goals... or change the partner. Elizabeth Ducie counts herself lucky to be with the right person: "I have a wonderfully supportive husband who puts up with my moods, allows me to use him as a sounding board, puts a note of realism into all my plans, and laughs at me if I get cross. And he runs the house, which helps tremendously."

Remember, support from family can manifest in different ways. Gertrude Stein liked to look at cows during writing sessions, and would drive out into the countryside with her life partner, Alice B. Toklas. Toklas then helped out by gamely persuading a cow into Stein's line of vision.

Because I don't have children, I'm especially grateful to author Melissa Addey for adding her perspective on the influence of kids. She remembers, "Before kids I did write, in a very leisurely way. I took time to watch the cats on the internet and I procrastinated enormously over sending my writing out. I made progress but very slowly. Writing was a fulfilling and relaxing hobby. With kids on the horizon, however, I suddenly went into power mode."

Notably, Addey didn't succumb to the temptation to catch up on her sleep while her baby snoozed: "I designated the baby's naps as my creative time and spent them writing, thinking, developing new ideas." She also found the fortitude to shun repeater tasks (see Chapter 4): "I ignored anything and everything else that I 'should' have done (the house looked like a pigsty, I swear) and attended only to my writing. Tiny bits of time here and there do actually add up. I wrote a book, *100 Things to Do While Breastfeeding*, in just four months while doing just that."

And when the kids get a little older, Addey confirms my hunch that boundaries can, and must, be set to protect your writing time. She says, "Teach your kids to do 'quiet time': this is one hour where they play alone and quietly with anything that isn't likely to go horribly wrong (not painting and nowhere near the pond). My son did this when he stopped naps, aged about two and a half and has done it ever since."

Another author with extensive wisdom about balancing writing with family life is Jim Heskett. In *The Juggling*

Author, Heskett explains he "sneaks in bits and pieces" of writing. He adds, "Being able to switch between writer and parent in an instant is a skill that takes some practice." Initially, he says, it will be "discombobulating to bounce back and forth... But after you do it enough times, it gets easier."

It seems that Jane Austen's social circle was not widely aware she was a writer, usually stationed in the sitting room of her Chawton home. Visitors tended to arrive unannounced, leaving her to hide her papers and hastily begin sewing.

However, even if your friends know of your writing ambitions, they may nonetheless believe you have time on your hands. This is one of my hot buttons and I've worked hard to dispel the myth that I'm a lady of leisure or am available at short notice. Having a weekly plan (see Chapter 4) has been hugely helpful, and I defend my schedule rigorously. For example, I only schedule appointments or accept coffee invitations on certain afternoons. Remember, it's okay to tell someone you have a conflicting meeting. They don't need to know the other attendee is your keyboard.

You'll need to train friends who phone at random times that they'll most likely get voicemail during your work times. The most effective way to end a text conversation is not to respond until much later. And if you have the very valuable type of friend who feels close enough to you to drop by unannounced, that, I'm afraid, is a conversation you need to have. In her Happier podcast, author Gretchen Rubin suggests that such people may be content if you designate a special time to see them. That way, they are comforted they will get a piece of your attention, and are less likely to try to grab it at random times.

At the end of the day, we teach people how to treat us. Be clear with yourself how you want your schedule to be respected, and don't be afraid to have kind, respectful conversations to teach others what that means.

The rest of your life is important and there will be myriad occasions when your writing simply has to take a back seat. As long as you're putting in small, regular pieces of effort, and making gradual forward progress, don't worry too much about the overall pace and how quickly you can publish. You'll still be much further along than you were this time last year.

Harness Your Energy

In Chapter 1 we noted that your energy levels almost certainly vary at different times of day. A key tactic for balancing life and writing is to aim to protect your "prime time" for creative, strategic, and important tasks.

Chances are, you already have something else happening during the times when you're at your sparkling best. If your writing is important to you, work out how you can ask others (be it your boss or your family) to accommodate tweaks in your schedule. Remember, it never hurts to ask, especially if you approach the conversation thoughtfully. Come prepared with ways this could benefit them too, or concessions you're willing to offer in return.

Similarly, if you're exhausted after dinner, that's a great time to fold laundry and listen to a light podcast. But be on your guard for anything that could fire you up and make it hard to sleep. Many people shouldn't exercise right before bed, and even innocuous social media surfing could ignite a strong reaction to news or someone else's views.

Use Your Ears

Do you wish you had more time to read, or stay up to date with industry information? Be sure to experiment with audiobooks and podcasts when you're exercising alone, traveling on public transport, or doing mundane household chores. The same goes for driving, but *only* if you can do so safely. I can attest that during gripping passages of a thriller, my attention to the road definitely wavers. It just isn't worth putting yourself or others in danger through distracted listening.

I don't recommend listening to other people's words when you're writing, working at your day job, or aiming to be present for your loved ones. Multitasking to that extent is damaging, not helpful. Neither job will get done well and you'll dramatically increase your sense of stress and time scarcity.

If you've never listened to audiobooks before, allow a little time to get used to this different way of "reading." It goes without saying, some narrators are better than others, and some choose to interpret the author's words with greater or lesser emotion. If you can't stand one voice, try a few others.

Some people like to listen to books and podcasts at 1.5 times or double speed. You might give this a try for nonfiction to see if you like it. I'm not sure most novels are suited to this: if you're going to absorb another author's words, give yourself the chance to really appreciate them.

Curve Balls

I've already asserted that I doubt "be an indie author" is your sole responsibility. Chances are, you're paying bills with another source of income, or doing vital work caring for others. Or both. So as writers, we need to expect that life will throw other, more pressing problems in our direction.

One mistake I kept making was to plan my time with no allowance for "curve balls." Instead of sketching out your week or visualizing your day with the ideal scenario of when you'll get time to write, you'll save your sanity if you expect the unexpected. Assume you'll lose at least one quality writing session to *something*, whether it's a sick child, broken washing machine, or flat tire. If life is kind to you and nothing untoward happens, great. But, chances are, it will.

For most of us, the reality is that unforeseen annoyances are actually to be anticipated. I've been much happier since I made a degree of peace with that fact.

Jackie Bouchard applies an even wiser attitude to irritants. She says, "Whenever I have to deal with something I don't want to, I just remember that everything is book fodder."

Great News About the Rest of Your Life

Don't despair about the avalanche of "other life" which appears to swamp your writing time. These contrasting activities provide valuable diversity to protect your energy and creativity.

Authors who have the luxury of being able to write all day will often take a full eight hours to achieve what you can do with one. For the human brain, knowing you have all day to do something can often result in precisely that.

And particularly if you are a parent, Melissa Addey's encouragement is nothing short of uplifting: "Over and over again I've personally experienced, seen or heard evidence that... having children brings with it a huge burst of creativity, a surge of entrepreneurial spirit leading to developing new material, increased output and achieving bigger dreams than might have been thought possible."

Summary

Writers without other responsibilities are in a tiny minority. With practice and mindfulness, you can grow your skills in making use of crumbs of time, riding the waves of your energy levels, and employing careful multitasking to listen to books during dull moments. Thoughtful, loving conversations with your family and friends will pay dividends if you stick to your guns clearly but kindly. And be honest when you yourself are your own worst thief of time. Avoid harsh self-criticism, but gently ease yourself back to the truly important tasks in your author life.

Self-Reflection Questions

1) Where are there some small pockets of time in your life which you could apply toward writing?

2) Can you identify one novel, nonfiction book, or podcast you'd like to listen to, and the best part of your day to do so?

3) Do you need to have, or revisit, any conversations with family and friends about the boundaries you desire in order to write?

4) What did you do today with your highest and lowest energy moments? What might you change about the type of tasks you undertake at different times?

Chapter 10: Dealing With Feeling Overwhelmed

There's no point sugarcoating this: as an indie author, you have an astonishing amount to juggle. Not only are there dozens of tasks you must complete in order to publish quality work, but you will be constantly bombarded by suggestions of things you *could* do.

Some of these bright ideas will come from friends who have no clue about independent publishing. Some will come from other authors, in the form of "this worked for me and I loved it," or possibly, "I haven't finished my own book yet, but I'm certain you should do this..." And many more suggestions will come from your online interactions and reading.

So here's the thing: you don't have to do it all and you shouldn't even try. You'll drive yourself crackers if you do. Know that as a self-starter (and I reckon if you're reading this, you are), you are particularly prone to taking on too much and then later facing an overwhelmed slump.

When this happens to Elizabeth Ducie, she relies on this fallback tactic: "When it all gets a bit overwhelming, I shut everything else out and concentrate on *the one thing* that has to be done first."

I have listed below some additional ways of crawling back out from under what's swamping you, to rescue your sense of ease.

Use Checklists

If you intend to publish more than one book, you'll find certain tasks need to be repeated. But depending on your pace of writing, editing, and publishing, you might only need to do some things once every two years. Don't waste time reinventing the wheel on each iteration, and save yourself the frustration of hitting a snag and dimly recalling that it tripped you up last time around. And even if you have just one book on your author shelf, many promotional tasks benefit from checklists.

Heather Wardell is a big fan of this approach. She says, "I have self-published 19 books and yet I'll still use my checklists for the next one. Thinking you can keep every detail of how to get an ISBN, the weird formatting tricks each retailer requires, and where you need to update your profiles when you've got a new book in your head is foolish."

To create these patterns where you can spend your time implementing, not thinking, checklists are your friend. It's wonderfully reassuring for your brain to have steps to follow, enabling you to move through routine tasks smoothly, then get on with the harder creative work.

Checklists I Use

Visit the bonus downloads for this book, if you'd like copies of examples of my lists:
- Title announcement and pre-order phase
- Pre-launch and launch phases
- Reviewing a printed proof

Note that I don't follow my lists slavishly. I might not do some items for every launch, for example. But it's a great comfort to my brain to know I've covered the necessary bases, or at least not forgotten any key tasks.

Avoid Email Overload

Email is someone else's opinion of how you should spend your time.

I adore that mantra and recite it at every opportunity.

You'd be an unusual indie author if you didn't want to stay connected to industry trends, improve your writing and business skills, keep in touch with other authors, enter a few giveaways, and absorb big news in your genre. But most of us get far too much email, and the number of newsletters we end up subscribed to can be dizzying. Apart from the time it takes you to read them all, they are incubators of distractions (see Chapter 5) and encourage us to over-compare (see Chapter 15).

The best tactic, of course, is to unsubscribe from as many updates as possible. I use this test for every single newsletter email: *Did this issue deliver value to me?* If not, I hit unsubscribe, and I exhort myself not to be upset when people do the same in response to my missives. Alternatively, you could create email rules to send them directly to a folder, and allow yourself 30 minutes of "tired" time, once a week, to browse through them. Regardless of your email reading habits, if you repeatedly find you delete a certain type of message without reading it, that's a strong clue that you should consider unsubscribing.

Above all else, remember how many lost words of your own writing it's costing you to read someone else's marketing message.

Slow Down

This is counterintuitive. As an intrepid indie author, you're probably extremely action-oriented. But because of that personality type, by setting yourself nominal deadlines (for example, finish this draft by July... publish this book by November...) you also create pressure, which is a key ingredient of feeling overwhelmed.

Bill Gates reckons most people consistently overestimate what we can achieve in a year. But, here's his good news: we underestimate what we can achieve in ten. So, if you're making solid, meaningful progress with your writing goals, ease up! Take some pressure off yourself and know that all forward motion is worthwhile.

One of the joys of publishing independently is that you ultimately control the pace. If you need to release your memoir in February instead of December, and if your book will be better because of those extra eight weeks, don't hesitate to slow down your timetable.

Unplug

If you've got so much on your to-do list you don't know which way to turn, or if your brain feels like it will implode from the competing priorities swirling around, try unplugging from the internet for a few days. You can still write, if you want to, but take a break from email, web research, and social media. Assuming your nearest and dearest still have a way to reach you, the rest of the world can wait.

You might want to schedule periodic "Airplane Days," as I call them, where you switch your equipment to airplane mode to create conditions for quality, thoughtful work. Set an "out of office" autoresponder for emails, and relish in your digital solitude. Sue Johnson goes so far as to say, "Get away from technology whenever you can."

Even if you don't embrace the notion of totally unplugging, try removing social media apps and games from your phone. Precious pockets of time (like waiting to pick up your kids, riding on the bus, or cooking dinner) can be used instead to read, write, meditate, or be fully present with your family. Jim Heskett says in *The Juggling Author*, "I removed all the stupid tappy tappy games from my phone. After a couple days, I didn't miss them anymore."

Give this a test drive—after all, you can always restore apps if you're desolate without them. Nonetheless, I promise your book sales won't plummet if you reduce, and get more intentional with, the time you spend on your phone.

Unplugging might feel like an emergency measure but it's not as drastic as it sounds. In any case, you can probably avoid the need to pull the plug if you prioritize regular rest and self-care. Look back at Chapter 8 for a refresher on how to refresh.

Take a Break

If writing a book is a battle, then goals are like cannonballs. I love them for the power and propulsion they'll bring to your efforts. However, many indie authors already exhibit extraordinary levels of self-drive, which is why we choose this path in the first place, and why we can rely largely on our own impetus to get things done. A downside of this personality trait is we can be terrible slave drivers, berating ourselves mercilessly when we feel we're not making progress quickly enough. So, if you have a tendency to transform sometimes into your own worst boss, know there will be periods when you *must* give yourself a break.

One of my favorite books on productivity is Moran and Lennington's *The 12 Week Year*, which divides the year into four portions. If you've spotted that a quarter of a year is, in fact, 13 weeks, not 12, that's because in each cycle, the 13th week is used for rest. It's a great structure and well worth remembering. Equally, some writers find that planning intentional fallow time into their publishing process, for example, between your first draft and editing phase, works especially well.

Revisit Chapter 8 for the merits of breaks of varying lengths. Goals are wonderful, but don't let them become a ball and chain around your ankle. Give yourself permission to play hooky sometimes.

Summary

The self-motivating, goal-oriented personality traits which make us ideally suited to become indie authors are the very same attributes which can cause us to take on too much, put onerous commitments on our own shoulders, and eventually droop through becoming overwhelmed. Recognizing this goes a long way toward protecting you from that dejection. In addition, you can utilize checklists, prune your inbox, and learn to expect the unexpected in your schedule. There is no shame in slowing down, or even unplugging from constant connectivity, if your mind becomes overly muddled.

Self-Reflection Questions

1) What types of checklists would you find helpful in your author activities? Start making them now.

2) Next time you view your email inbox, how many messages can you find which would be candidates for unsubscribing? Take particular aim at anything you delete without reading.

3) Have you ever taken an Airplane Day, or unplugged from the internet for a while? How did it feel? Would you benefit from scheduling this more regularly?

Chapter 11: Minimum Viable Product

As already stated, this book doesn't intend to be a comprehensive how-to self-publishing guide. I'm not an expert on every possible channel open to you and what's more, services change fast. I also believe that trying to understand every single option available as an indie author will slow you down, stress you out, and even lead to decision paralysis.

Instead, here are some minimum steps you *have* to do to release a quality book to the world. Notice that word *quality*: if you're not worried about that, you could already have published your book in less time than it's taken you to read this far. So I'm assuming you at least want to do your readers the courtesy of presenting them with polished, credible writing.

For any step in this process where you need to hire help, Chick Lit author Cat Lavoie recommends prudence. She has published four novels and says, "Do your homework and make sure you are spending wisely and are hiring the right person (editor, proofreader, formatter, cover designer, etc.) for the job. Check out their websites, get recommendations from writer friends or writer groups, and look up other novels they have worked on." Stefania Shaffer, who self-published a series for middle grade readers, believes you get what you pay for: "Publishing independently is not the time to buy labor on the cheap. Understand what is fair market value and how a freelancer operates and if you are a good fit together for your working styles and time frame, with a shared end result in mind."

Write Your Book

Why am I listing this insultingly obvious step? Because of all the people in the world who claim they want to publish a book, shockingly few have finished writing it. A popular figure quoted is that 200 million Americans aspire to being authors, so clearly many are stalling at that first hurdle. Before you get too hung up on the steps to publish your work, please, please, buckle down and write it.

Self-edit Like Crazy

You can do more than you might think in making your book great. Entire how-to guides are written on this topic alone, but options open to you include:
- Once you finish the first draft, write a blurb (not a synopsis) of what your book is about. Then reread. Have you created what you thought?
- Plot your scenes and narrative arc. How is the pace? What's happening at the 25%, 50%, and 75% points?
- Does every single scene add something? What's different at the end of the scene? If nothing, you should consider cutting it.
- Print your manuscript out and see if editing on paper reveals nuances you'd missed on a screen.
- Similarly, read it aloud.
- Read it backwards, if you have the patience.
- Cut words. Pretend your book is a telegram and you're paying per word. Search for words you overuse (and see my own list of words to cull in the bonus resources). Force yourself to cull.
- Spell check it. Yes, really.

Jackie Bouchard believes, "The number one way readers end up buying books is through word-of-mouth recommendations... so the best thing you can do is write the best book you can write!"

Get Critique From Beta Readers

Once you've done the best job you can on your own, it's time to get serious, comprehensive feedback on your book.

Other writers make ideal beta readers but, especially the first time around, recruit enough people so that you cover your bases if some are too harsh, some too lenient, and some don't actually complete the reading and send you feedback. Trusted friends might be fine too, but they are less likely to give you the feedback you truly need. They'll either be too kind, too vague, or miss the point and want to tell you all about their own not-yet-started book.

My favorite source of beta readers is my writing tribe (see Chapter 7). Even then, you'll need to be precise about what you are looking for. Send them specific questions (find mine in the bonus downloads) and be clear that they need to be *honest*. Let them know what you don't want, too: tell them not to spend precious time finding typos as you'll be hiring a proofreader later.

Do allow time after the beta read to make whatever changes are necessary. I've seen authors commit to an imminent publication date *before* their book goes to beta readers. This is a sign that you're not willing to rip the book apart if your beta readers tell you it's needed, and is actually a subtle way of signaling to your beta crew that you think the book is mostly "just fine" already.

In the past I've offered to pay beta readers but I no longer do so. I aim to trade this service with other authors, and we rely on each other to be trustworthy and thorough. By offering small payments I believe I attracted some beta readers who read as quickly as possible and gave minimal feedback, just to collect their reward. It's much better to have people who genuinely believe in your work and will look to you to reciprocate when their own books are ready.

Craft a Gorgeous Cover

A stunning, professional quality cover needs to be on your must-have list. It's not optional. Nothing will kill your book's chances faster than an amateurish effort, or one that's beautiful but wrong for your genre.

I do think it's worth educating yourself on effective covers for your niche; you should be able to spot some patterns pretty fast. At the time of writing, I love my fiction book covers but they're not quite right for romantic comedy. Take a look at them and you'll see the colors are good, but the overall look is too clean and uncluttered: most others in this genre feature intricate illustrations and swirling, flowery borders. One of the best places to view an assortment of covers and a professional critique is Joel Friedlander's monthly cover design awards on his site, The Book Designer. Become a regular visitor here and you'll soon develop a taste for what works and what doesn't.

You might even enjoy trying to guess, from the cover alone, whether a book is traditionally or independently published. That can be a revealing exercise.

Some of the most beautiful covers I've seen recently are for Alina Sayre's middle grade fantasy series, The Voyages of the Legend. She says, "Cover art was the biggest financial investment I made in my books, and I'm so glad I did! For better or worse, people do judge books by their covers... I can't overstate how important cover art has been to the success of my books. Also, make sure that your designer is not only good at what they do, but easy to work with. Making a book cover involves a fair amount of stress and trust."

And it's not just novels which need first-rate covers, as Elizabeth Lovick will attest. "Give careful thought to the cover—it is as important in nonfiction as it is in fiction. A good graphic artist will pay for themselves several times over!"

We agree, then, your cover is crucial, but you can be creative about how you get one that's top-notch. If you don't have much eye for it, yes, as Lovick says, you'll need to hire someone. Otherwise, you might be able to give direction to a willing friend with graphic design skills. Don't forget you'll need similar but different cover files for your ebook and paperback, if you decide to do both. Because the paperback is actually printed, rather than just seen on a screen, the cover file needs to be a dramatically higher image resolution, so that it doesn't appear fuzzy or jagged. Also, take great care with the placement of the spine and back cover components, such as space for the barcode.

Remember, indie authors have the enormous advantage of being able to change our book covers easily. If you publish and later suspect your cover design is dragging your book's performance down, update it.

Make Your Blurb Brilliant

Another common peeve of mine with book quality is the back cover blurb. Only the front cover is more important in convincing a reader to give your work a try. Even if you've written a terrific book, you may need help crafting an enticing blurb.

For fiction, your biggest pitfall is summarizing the plot of your novel. You should be able to set up the situation and the main character's problem to overcome, and leave a dangling question of whether they'll prevail. If you find yourself revealing any plot point which happens more than about 20% of the way into your novel, you're giving a synopsis, not a teaser.

For nonfiction, the key benefits and takeaways for the reader need to stand loud and proud in your blurb.

Your community of author friends, and beta readers, can help enormously in crafting the description which goes on your cover. The good news is, if you are still struggling, paying for professional help in blurb writing shouldn't break the bank.

Pay a Proofreader

People can argue about what constitutes great writing, and covers are largely a matter of personal taste, but a typo is a typo. If you invest in nothing else, you must pay for professional proofreading, out of respect to your readers. Not doing so is like not washing your face before you go to a party.

A good proofreader won't be cheap, and you should take care to find someone who truly has the professional skills needed for this task, *not* a friend with sharp eyes or a struggling author who has branched out. Tracey Gemmell learned this lesson: "Many authors in self-publishing team up with other authors with regards to editing and proofreading. Exchanging skills can cut costs tremendously. But quality matters, and there is risk to cutting corners. Trust me on that one."

I am an incredibly picky reader—I'm blushing to admit I've been known to send other indie authors an unsolicited list of corrections—but I'm not professionally trained, and my proofreaders always find hundreds of mistakes. Bestselling author and marketing specialist Guy Kawasaki has related a similar tale, when he thought his first book was essentially perfect, yet received it back from his proofreader with corrections spilling off the page.

Please, please don't skip this task. It's devastating to see a typo in the first line of an indie author's published work. And if I spot three errors in the first chapter, I'm probably going to knock a star off my Amazon review, on principle.

Your readers are entitled to debate the artistic merit in the words you choose, and whether or not you're a "good" writer. But typos and punctuation slips are unequivocal. If you don't care enough about your own work to want it to be correct, then please take the proofreading step on behalf of every other author who will be tarred by the same sloppy brush.

And having made this investment, be especially careful as you work through your manuscript accepting or rejecting the changes your eagle-eyed proofreader has made. My own experience is that this is a key time when I introduce further errors into the book.

Lastly, if your project is nonfiction, you might also need a specialist pair of eyes. Elizabeth Lovick can't afford for her readers to encounter errors in her knitting patterns. She says, "If you are doing anything technical in any way, get a Technical Editor (TechEd) to go over your explanations, numbers etc. Find an editor who knows their stuff."

Format Reasonably Well

You're probably forming the (correct) opinion that I'm a perfectionist. However, formatting is an area where you do get a little leeway. Basically, you should aim for your book to be well enough formatted that readers won't notice. Yes, a publishing professional might spot issues, and I've even seen whole training sessions on how to make your book indistinguishable from a traditionally published one, but this really is an area where good enough is... good enough!

If you're publishing using Amazon KDP or Smashwords, they both provide plenty of handholding on formatting and will notify you of errors. If you're comfortable working with long documents and styles in your word processing software, there's no reason why you shouldn't be able to get through the formatting requirements on your own. However, there are plenty of people who will format for you and since costs are reasonable, this might be one area where outside help is well worth it. To check they know what they're doing, ask them how they deal with places where you've used three dots (...) instead of an ellipsis (…), and whether they incorporate * * (non-breaking space) in their work.

For your ebook, review it to make sure it's good enough and pay particular attention to your front and back matter and any links you've included there. But don't drive yourself nuts trying to check every page at every font size on every possible reading device: it's not necessary and you'll be a nervous wreck by publication day. Trust me, I've tried!

In general, readers are more forgiving of the odd formatting quirk in an ebook than in a paperback, and if you're publishing a printed edition, you should take special care with this. Unlike the ebook, where every device does its best to display your words to the reader according to its own size constraints and their reading preferences, a paperback gives you the opportunity to control exactly what goes where. This means you can, and should, check every single page. Your cover design also needs to step up a level (see above). One of the most common mistakes I see in self-published paperbacks is not having a wide enough inner margin. It's an annoying reading experience to destroy the spine of a book in order to see the edges: watch out for this in your proof copy, and be prepared to go around the proof cycle again if you're not happy.

Ideally, your paperback should have a different header on odd and even pages (for example, the book title on one side and your name on the other). You'll need to be pretty good with page styles to pull this off, and readers probably won't notice. They might, however, be alert to other slips, like including page numbers on chapter start pages and blank pages. You don't want headers on chapter start pages (or front and back matter)—they look weird. Pick a traditional book off your bookshelf and you'll see these "rules" in action. You can also get a more professional result by checking (and fudging if necessary) that you don't end up with tiny fragments of text falling to a fresh page at the end of a chapter. And if you fancy a few swirls as section breaks, or a beautiful font as a chapter header, the paperback is your playground.

Remember, unlike the ebook, cheating a little with blank lines, word spacing or page breaks to finalize an attractive paperback layout is perfectly fine. Don't, whatever you do, try the same tricks with your ebook: step away from this beautifying urge and let the reader's device do the best it can with minimal formatting.

Buy Your ISBN

Much has been written about whether you should purchase your own International Standard Book Number or allow a publishing services company to take care of that for you. You'll want to do a little of your own research, but the overwhelming advice from self-publishing experts is that it's well worth investing in your own ISBN.

This small administrative step will ensure that *you* are listed as the publisher, not the printing company you use. You'll control the metadata which describes your book and aids its discovery, and you'll keep your options open if you decide to change your supplier of print copies in the future.

At the time of writing, $295 gets you a block of ten ISBNs. Since you'll need a different ISBN for different formats (like print, ebook, and audio), this sets you up for your first book and one or two beyond.

Publish on Amazon as an Ebook

In the spirit of *minimum viable publishing*, releasing your ebook on Amazon gets the job done. It's there, online, for sale. Your friends and family can buy it, you've published, you can check the box on your bucket list. And since my aim with this guide is to reduce stress and overload, you don't *have* to put yourself through any further effort.

Now, whether it's a good idea *only* to publish on Amazon is the subject of massive debate. And by "good idea," we need to balance good for you, good for your reader, and good for the long-term prospects of the book industry.

On the one hand, it's the simplest way to publish and if you give Amazon exclusive rights to your ebook, you'll enjoy certain benefits. For example, at the time of writing, readers can borrow your book as well as buying it, and you can also run free promotions under certain constraints. But by doing that, you're also handing considerable power to Amazon. After all, they're a zealous, sophisticated for-profit business, not an author incubator. As their market dominance grows, and competition gets squeezed out, it's easy to imagine their terms for authors will become much less favorable. Your 70% royalty could shrink to 60%, 30%, or lower, and if no viable alternatives have survived, there may not be much you can do about it. Your readers, too, might not all want to get their ebooks from Amazon. You might prefer to publish on other platforms in order to meet them where they're browsing.

I'm currently with KDP Select (the exclusive Amazon option) and I admit it bothers me. Financially, though, I make far more money from readers *borrowing* my books than *buying* them. If I were to make my ebooks available through other outlets, my short-term income would be devastated.

So, you should know that the simple, easy choice may have significant long-term implications. Whatever you decide (and you can experiment with being exclusive or not), just be mindful of the risks involved. By all means keep it simple, but make that a mindful choice, not a default.

Publish a Paperback (Maybe)

As a first-time author, there's a strong likelihood you'll want the thrill of seeing your book in print. If you want to have a launch party, convince a bookstore to let you do a signing, or hold other live events, then offering a paperback makes strong sense. Many people prefer physical books when buying gifts, and you'll probably find that offering signed physical books as a giveaway prize is more popular than the opportunity to win an ebook.

Cat Lavoie says that for her, "There's nothing better than holding a physical copy of your novel in your hands. Even if most people read my work on Kindles or tablets, I need to know that readers who want to read a 'real' book can get one. One of my writer dreams is to see a stranger with their nose buried in one of my books on my morning subway commute."

The demographics of your target audience are crucial, too. Fantasy author Alina Sayre says, "In marketing to middle grade readers, I've had vastly superior success with selling print books. I think this comes from two main causes. First, not every kid has access to an e-reader (and not every parent wants their kid sitting down in front of yet another screen). Second, print books are not just a reading experience, but a social experience. A big part of my marketing work is doing writing workshops in schools and running booths at literary festivals. Sometimes I'm the first 'real live author' a kid has ever met, and they want me to sign their print book. Then the book becomes not only something they can read and enjoy, but something to help them remember that big moment."

Compared with just publishing an ebook, you'll incur extra costs in formatting the paperback and cover design, and a few extra headaches in making it look beautiful. However, these tend to be forgotten once your shipment of books arrives on your doorstep. In case you didn't already know, these days print on demand technology means you can order just a few copies, instead of filling every spare corner of your home with books you hope to sell one day.

All that said, you don't have to publish a paperback and you may choose not to. In some genres, ebook sales now *crush* physical sales. Romance is one, and I suspect any genre where keen readers devour high volumes of books and expect low prices will be the same. To get a sense for these genres, look at the ebook only or "digital first" arms of traditional publishers. My romantic comedies, for example, sell very few paperbacks, except in December when there's a noticeable bump in sales for gifts.

These days, publishing a paperback is at your discretion, and you certainly don't have to do it at the same time your ebook is released.

Summary

Publishing your book is a key time to be mindful about where you really need to spend time and effort to ensure a quality outcome. You can avoid paying for superfluous services, but don't skimp on minimum standards. You *do* need to invest in professional proofreading and strong cover design.

The decision on whether to publish an ebook, or paperback, or both, is in your hands and is not final. You can do one format, then add the other when you're ready. Many authors consider holding their physical book in their hands to be one of the most joyful moments of indie publishing.

Self-Reflection Questions

1) Have you done the best possible job you can of writing and self-editing your book?

2) Have you recruited the right beta readers, who will give you honest, kind, and actionable feedback? And have you allowed sufficient time to truly consider, then implement, their recommendations?

3) Have you invested in minimum professional services (proofreading, formatting, cover design) to be courteous to your readers and represent the indie author movement well?

4) Is it important to you to publish an ebook, paperback, or both? Why?

Chapter 12: Minimum Viable Marketing

Just as the whiz kids of Silicon Valley love to launch with a Minimum Viable Product to test the market and provide momentum for further iterations, I believe the concept of Minimum Viable Marketing is crucial for indie authors.

We're so lucky that in today's connected world, there are dozens, if not hundreds of ways to promote your book. There are entire books, blogs, podcasts, and side hustles devoted to this topic. And for every imaginable tactic, you'll find an author who is a fan, extolling its virtues, and claiming it worked like magic for them.

And that's the problem. There's so much you *could* be doing, that your marketing action list can get out of hand incredibly quickly. Even if you truly adore book promotion (and let's face it, few authors do), the array of options robs you of your writing time. And if you try to do a little bit of everything, you'll run yourself ragged and not do any of it very well. As with so many aspects of being an indie author, the answer is to focus. Elizabeth Lovick suggests, "Work out your *modus vivendi* before you start. Work out exactly who will want your book, where they buy books from, how you will market it."

Knowing your intended audience is key, and once you can picture that person, move forward with these four things.

Your Four Essential Marketing Pillars

Get just four aspects of marketing lined up and you can pat yourself on the back that you have a solid foundation. Later, maybe you'll build on it, but don't get distracted by other opportunities until you have at least these.

Website

It's been said you don't *absolutely* need a website in order to get started, but the reality is, most indie authors will want their own web presence sooner or later.

Unless you know for sure this is your only book (refer to the aspirations you identified in Chapter 3), create an author site, not a book site. By that, I mean you should register *paulinewiles.com* not *savingsaffronsweeting.com*. And do register your own domain name, don't settle for *paulinewiles.wordpress.com* or similar.

Although you may need to pay for help to get your website set up, do aim to understand enough about your site that you can make basic edits yourself. Paying someone every time you want to write a blog post or add a speaking event to your site will ruin your author profits.

The minimum pages you need on your site are:
- **Home page**: Aim for clean, simple and attractive. Include links to any other social media profiles here too.
- **Contact information**: Don't make people fill out a form to reach you. Agents, journalists, bloggers, and everyone else who might want to get hold of you hate it, so just list your contact information. The exception is if you're also a book reviewer, when you'll probably want a form to gather the necessary information which accompanies a review request. Keep it simple and don't make readers jump through hoops.
- **Books/writing**: One or more pages to describe your published or upcoming work, and/or any articles you've published. A cover image, blurb, and some buy links are all that you need here.
- **Email newsletter signup**: Put this on its own page but consider featuring it, or pop-ups, in other locations too. It's imperative you collect email addresses (with appropriate permissions) directly,

instead of relying on Facebook, Instagram or other social media to reach fans.

You can, of course, have far more pages, but a small simple site is a thousand times better than no site at all. Get this done, don't get hung up on perfection. If you enjoy blogging and will update it regularly, add that feature too, but it's by no means necessary.

You'll save yourself time down the road if you create a stylesheet for your online branding. This doesn't need to be complicated: identify two or three fonts which will represent you (make sure you're not infringing copyright by using them), and four to five colors (at most). Record the RGB and Hex codes for those colors, as you'll need them time and time again. For color inspiration, look at successful book covers in your genre and aim for a similar feel. A gritty crime writer, for example, won't benefit from a lilac background on her website. In the same folder on your computer, store your author headshot(s) and any logos you use frequently. In time, you may want to make these available on your website as a media kit, but it's certainly not a necessity at first. Having your colors and logos handy will help you maintain consistency when creating images or sending email communications.

Suggested Tools

As discussed in the introduction, this book *does not* set out to be a guide to tools for self-publishers. If you're looking for a comprehensive listing of your options, I recommend Carla King's *A Consumer's Guide for Self-Publishers: Writing & Publishing Tools and Services*, available via the Self-Pub Boot Camp.

Tools like Wix are available such that you can literally put a site together in a couple of hours, for free. I started off coding websites in the days of HTML and FTP programs, so I was initially suspicious of a service like this which claims to make everything pretty for you and your viewers. But, I've seen some really nice pages through Wix and having any website is better than none.

Like millions of other business owners, I use WordPress and if you're serious about your writing career, I'd suggest you aim for a self-hosted WordPress site (not a free one). You'll pay an annual hosting fee, but it's worth it to control your own piece of online real estate.

Whether you choose WordPress or another option, know that you (or somebody you designate) needs to apply updates, including for any features such as plug-ins. Otherwise, you're at real risk of being hacked. I learned that lesson the hard way.

Email Newsletter

I beg you, don't overlook this author must-have. Regardless of the size of your audience through social media channels, having permission to land directly in a reader's inbox is priceless. Too many authors lament losing (free) access to their large online following as a result of an algorithm change. You *must* be able to talk to your fans without being held to ransom by a social media provider. By the way, if the process of writing and sending a newsletter is so scary that you're using that as an excuse not to set up a list, *create the list anyway*, and worry about the newsletter later.

Once you've started collecting email addresses of people who'd like to hear from you, ideally you should start talking to them. Depending on your level of technical comfort, you might want to get some help creating your first newsletter (refer to your website stylesheet here, it will be a big help in creating the look and feel) but you should aim to learn enough to be able then to replicate your first campaign for future communications.

Clearly, whenever you release a new book or have special news, you'll want to notify your list. Authors sometimes struggle with content for newsletters between releases, and if you are reluctant to add yet more to the inboxes of your fans, you might feel comfortable only writing when you publish new work. Nonetheless, some indie authors do a terrific job of regular contact. If you'd like to see a strong example, I suggest you sign up for Lisa Manterfield's news.

If you do want to email between releases, you could consider:
- Teaming up with other authors to offer giveaways.
- Linking back to popular posts on your blog.
- A contest to name a character in your Work in Progress.
- A contest to name a place in your Work In Progress.
- Inviting readers to challenge you to come up with a piece of flash fiction featuring three words they supply.
- Recommending something you just read.
- Highlighting another author you enjoy.
- Introducing them to one of your social media accounts.
- Asking for help with reviews or spreading the word.

Suggested Tools

Your website designer or virtual assistant may push you heavily in the direction of their preferred email newsletter service. That's fine, but do ask them what your monthly cost will be and whether they are an affiliate (making money from you signing up). I've seen author friends paying steep monthly fees for a service that's simply too sophisticated for their needs.

I love MailChimp because it's free up to a large number of subscribers (2000 at the time of writing), and if you get past that number, that counts as a "nice problem to have." MailChimp offers an impressive range of free features, like sending automatic welcome messages to new subscribers. The downside, for me, is that they tend to change their user interface quite often, so you may find it looks unfamiliar every time you log in.

MailChimp is certainly not the only way of administering your mailing list. Just make sure that the method you pick helps you manage people who unsubscribe and keeps you within the law.

Once you've chosen an email service provider, be sure to add the code which they supply to the newsletter signup page on your website. If you want to get more fancy, you can do pop-up forms and so on, but one basic place for readers to subscribe is the minimum you should aim for.

One Social Media Channel

As an author, your main job is to write your book, or write your next book. Social media is a comfort and resource as well as a marketing tool, but it can also be a tremendous time suck, luring you into the belief you're "working" when in fact your manuscript is gathering dust (see Chapter 5). So to get started, make a list of the social media channels you *enjoy* using. Now make a list of the places you believe your ideal reader hangs out online. If you're not sure, ask one or two early fans. Finally, pick just one channel which appears in both lists, and devote your efforts there.

As Wendy Janes says, "Resist the pressure to be everywhere at once. Find the social media platforms that feel right for you." Tempting as it might feel, you *do not* need to be on every platform. For Janes, that platform is Twitter: "You don't have to be an expert in social media from the outset. Like so many useful things in life, it's a learning curve. To me the Twittersphere feels like one big cocktail party—it's always great to meet new people and to catch up with old friends too."

Make sure your profile is attractive and informative and pay attention to the mix of your posts: share useful/entertaining content, and help promote others too. I particularly enjoy using Twitter to support other authors and show interest in their work, providing a little cheerleading when appropriate. Or, as Janes puts it, "Join social media to make friends, not to make money."

If your work has a distinctive subject matter, that can provide your ideal angle for social media. With canines featuring in every novel she writes, Jackie Bouchard loves this approach: "If you're like me and don't want to hype your books/yourself, try to find something else within the themes of your writing that you can connect with readers over. My social media posts are 90% focused on dogs. Via my love of dogs, I connect with other dog lovers, and then I just hope they're also booklovers!"

However, even being on just one social media channel can have its pitfalls. Let's look at those now.

Social Media Pitfall 1: Lost Time

While I was finalizing *Saving Saffron Sweeting*, it was not uncommon for me to spend an hour every morning just "processing" my social media feeds, following links, reading articles, and sharing. Let's put that in context: at 360 hours a year, that's nine full working weeks lost.

So, I strongly suggest you set a time budget for using social media: how many days per week will you visit, and for how long each session? If you enjoy it, once a day is probably enough for social media. And please, slot it in when you're tired and generally unproductive, not during prime writing time. If you don't especially enjoy it, drop down to three times a week. Set a timer and be social, engaging, and supportive. Then close that browser and get on with your life. Otherwise, you'll find hours drift away.

Think hard before installing the app on your phone and do look into tools like Buffer or Recurpost which let you schedule some of your content in advance.

Social Media Pitfall 2: Focus

Social media has seductive powers to distract you from your key priorities. For example, you're supposed to be editing your book, but when you come across a tantalizing webinar about driving traffic to your site through Pinterest, will you resist the lure?

Be wary, too, of keeping social media tabs open on your computer while you work: this will wreck your focus and is the perfect way to procrastinate when you can't quite think of the next sentence.

Social Media Pitfall 3: Comparisons

Chapter 15 highlights the damage to morale that too much comparison with others can cause. Know that the more time you spend on social media, the more exposed you'll be to other people's (apparent) successes. Heather Wardell has noticed this also: "It's so important to be an author your way, and yet so hard when the internet lets us see exactly what other authors are doing and who is successful." She reminds us too that, especially on social media, "not everything that gets posted is true."

Social Media Pitfall 4: Algorithm Changes

The more time you've invested in building your social media following, and the more audience you have there, the more vulnerable you are to changes in the platform's algorithm which determines how readily you can reach your audience. Always keep in mind, the owner of that platform can change the rules, and their charges, at the drop of a hat.

Suggested Tools

If you enjoy being active on social media, consider learning how to make basic images. Otherwise, it's a good investment to pay someone else make them. (This kind of task would be well suited to fiverr.com.) For authors, the skill of taking an existing image, like your book cover or an inspirational photo, and adding words (such as a price promotion or quote from your book) is key. For examples, author Cat Lavoie's Twitter feed is a rich source.

Two of the most popular tools for images are Canva and PicMonkey; there are many others up to and including fully featured graphic design packages like Photoshop. For your purposes, one of the free online tools should suffice.

Images you've created will also come in handy for your email newsletter, and for your profile pages on the social media platforms you use.

You can automate your social media posts with tools like Hootsuite and Buffer, but I'd suggest there's no substitute for visiting the platform in person, in order to respond to and engage with others. However, there's no harm in advance scheduling for some of the posts you yourself want to instigate, especially if you'd like these to go live during your high energy writing times.

A Support Network of Other (Indie) Authors

Based on what you read in Chapter 7, did you invest some time and effort in building your author tribe? If so, this group will likely form a vibrant part of your marketing efforts.

Indies are a positive bunch and if you cheerlead for them, they'll typically do the same for you. You can team up on giveaways, share marketing tips, and collaborate on innovative promotional projects. Fellow authors are among the most likely readers to take the time to review your book, as they understand the importance far more than your general acquaintances.

For this reason, I consider other authors to be one of my most powerful marketing assets. I warmly encourage you to nurture your own tribe of author friends and enjoy the wonderful alliances that can result.

So, those are your four essential marketing pillars. Now let's consider your book launch.

Make Your Launch Sparkle

There is no better time to promote a book than in the few weeks before and after its initial publication. Do the best possible job of releasing your book to the world and, if you categorically *must* burn any midnight oil, this would be the time to do it. However, this is *not* when you start your promotional thinking—ideally you'll start to get activities lined up many months ahead of publication.

Whatever you do, don't hurry your launch to hit an arbitrary date. It's far better to publish your book when it's ready and when advance readers have had a reasonable time to review it. Many blog tour organizers recommend a three-month lead time, if you want reviews ready for release day. If you choose to do a pre-order, it's even more important to hit your declared deadline of having tiptop files ready for upload to your chosen channels. See more on the pitfalls of rushing to publish in Chapter 13.

Your launch period might be a good time to hire a Virtual Assistant (VA), as you'll want to be active on your social media channels with the happy news, possibly accompanied by shareable quotes from your book, images, a book trailer, reader giveaway, and so on. Stefania Shaffer, who published a five-book series within an eight-month period says of her VA, "Mine saved me several times over from cradling myself in the fetal position beneath my desk."

If you work at a day job, do yourself a favor and take publication day off. Even if you're a great multitasker and manage a bit of book promotion during your work breaks, you'll find release day can keep you busy from early morning to late evening. You've earned this limelight, so make the mental bandwidth to enjoy it. And you might be lucky enough to have readers in many different time zones who are kind enough to talk about your book online, while you're asleep.

Be sure to pencil in some recovery time after your launch. Despite the best planning, you'll probably find the last few days before release a little frenetic (at least, you should, if you're doing a great job of quality checks and marketing). Once your book is out there, take a pause to celebrate and renew your energy for whatever project comes next. Recovery is essential to feeling you can continue on your author journey: without it, you'll fizzle like a marathon runner without water.

Don't Try to Be Everywhere

Just as important as the marketing you do choose are the options you consciously avoid. There are so many possibilities today for authors to promote their work that there will always be something else you could try, a method that's worked well for someone else, or a cool new social media site to join. But if you try to do everything—and keep in mind, marketing advice changes frequently—you'll end up exhausted, inefficient, and spread so thinly your efforts are diluted beyond hope. Every book is different and every author is different, so here are some smart ways to choose:

- Focus your marketing on what comes easily to you. For example, let's say you write how-to guides for cat owners. Do you love to use a tool like Canva to make shareable tips superimposed on feline images? Or would you have more fun visiting local pet stores and asking to host book signings?
- If a marketing option doesn't sound enjoyable, give it a miss. You'll stress yourself out and probably spend more time than necessary. For example, if you hate public speaking, don't try to visit local groups with your history novel. If you can't think of a single topic, don't try to start a blog. Don't feel you have to join lots of Goodreads groups—unless you want to.
- Even if an activity is enjoyable, is it a good use of your time? For example, attending a book fair might involve four hours of driving and demolish a whole day. Know that you could have spent that time

writing your *next* book, and weigh the opportunity accordingly. But, check what you said is most important to you (see Chapter 3). If it's always been your dream to hold a signing in an independent bookstore, by all means, invest the time to make that happen. Just make sure a friend has a camera to capture the highlights.
- Keep an eye on what's effective. I no longer bother with press releases for my novels. Nor was Wattpad a worthwhile platform for me. But these two might be dynamite for you.
- In deciding what's worth repeating, know how you'll measure marketing effectiveness. For example, do you want to see a positive Return on Investment (ROI) for every paid promotion, or is building awareness and reaching new readers okay by you? I tend to look solely at ROI: if I pay $30 for an advert, and I'm making $1 per sale, I want to see sales bump up by at least 30 that day. But other authors take a much longer term view.

Assuming you've done a quality job with your first book and readers like it, then remember this advice from Bella Andre, a bestselling indie author with seven million sales under her belt: "The best marketing you can do is to write the next book."

Reviews Rule!

If you're still in doubt about where to spend your marketing energy, focus on getting reviews from readers. Not only are these wonderful in convincing others to give you a try, but when you want to try a paid promotion, the best advertisers will insist (either explicitly or implicitly) on a minimum number of reviews. And the boost you'll feel when a complete stranger gives your book five stars is colossal.

Tips for Getting Reviews

You should only ever aim to acquire authentic, honest reviews. Don't compromise on integrity, and play your part in keeping reviews trustworthy and useful for your readers.

- Make (or ask your Virtual Assistant to create) a short review request document. You can get a sample of mine in the bonus downloads. Including this document with your request will come across as more professional and more respectful.
- Research which bloggers have reviewed books similar to yours. Not only does this increase the chances they'll accept yours for review, but it dramatically raises the odds that they'll like it! *Do not* simply blast your book to every blog which has ever reviewed anything.
- Always follow the contact preferences posted on the blog (for example, tweeting to the blogger is rarely cool) and allow lots of time. Use their name in your email if you possibly can and mention how you found them, or another review of theirs you enjoyed.
- Keep careful track of the bloggers you approach and who says yes. After a reasonable time, you'll want to follow up politely if they promised to review but have not yet managed to do so.
- And, as is often suggested, be sure to add an author's note to the end of your book letting readers know how important reviews are, and asking them to leave one.

Summary

Instead of trying to do as much book marketing as possible, aim for doing the best job you can in as few places as you can get away with. In other words, don't go broad, go deep. Your minimum marketing needs are a website, an email newsletter, one social media channel, and a support network of other authors. If you don't already have these four in place, prioritize them in this order: email list, support network, website, social media.

It's worth spending additional time making a big splash for your book's launch, and then in seeking honest, ethical reviews. Do these activities steadily and you'll not only see solid results, but you'll save yourself from burnout too.

Self-Reflection Questions

1) Do you have the four minimum pillars of marketing in place? If not, plan your actions in the priority order listed above.

2) What kinds of book promotion have you already tried? Did you achieve a positive Return on Investment, fresh reader engagement, or some other benefit? Make note of those you feel were effective and/or enjoyable, for future use.

3) What achievements did you list as most important in Chapter 3? Pick one which feels realistic for you at the current stage of your career. How could you make that happen?

4) Have you contacted at least 30 book bloggers to ask them to review your book? If not, start to make a list of appropriate blogs to reach out to.

Part 4: Stay Inspired

Chapter 13: The Easiest Pitfalls to Dodge

Nobody is claiming that being an indie author is easy, but there are a few classic pitfalls which you must dodge, both for your own sake and for your readers' sake. Chapter 11 explored how to avoid potential snags in the quality of your book and its cover design. This chapter describes some further pitfalls you should have on your radar.

Rushing It

One of the best traits of indie authors is we are action oriented and bring our work to market fast. But in your haste and excitement to share your book, rushing the process is a major and totally avoidable pitfall. Especially if this is the first or second time you're publishing, it's likely you'll underestimate how long some parts of the process take.

Don't put yourself under arbitrary pressure to hit a certain publication season, like Valentine's Day for romances, or December for general gift buying. There are scores of other books being released then: as an indie you may do better by not entering the fray. Also, the panic you're likely to feel as you scramble to check your book one last time only amplifies the exhaustion and potential anticlimax when you realize your precious work has not launched with the sales avalanche you hoped for. Feeling overwhelmed during the publishing process, followed by underwhelming revenues, are a key combination in making indies quit.

Equally, in all that rushing to publish, you're likely to overlook quality glitches in your book, blurb, sales page, or other marketing messages. Take your time and launch the best possible book you can, the first time around. Yes, these days it's fairly easy to republish, but why put yourself through that? The weeks before and after a book's initial release are incredibly precious. Use that time wisely and manage your energy accordingly.

Doing Nothing Because You Can't Do Everything

At every writing conference I attend, I see would-be authors looking like deer caught in headlights when they learn of all the publishing-related activities they "could" or "should" be doing. Unless you can clone yourself, or you have an astonishingly large budget for a Virtual Assistant, you will *never* be able to take care of every task recommended to you, or at least, not at the pace you'd like.

But equally, don't make the mistake of doing *nothing* because you can't do *everything*. Small steps, or a few minutes a day devoted to a bigger task, add up fast. Pat Edwards reminds us, "Don't think, 'I'm too slow.' I wrote my book with 20 minutes a day. I persisted with my schedule and less than a year later my book was complete."

Revisit Chapter 11 (Minimum Viable Product) and Chapter 12 (Minimum Viable Marketing). Do these tasks first, before getting sidetracked by other author activities. Also, I would argue, don't spend your precious money attending events where someone will attempt to add yet one more thing to your to-do list. Never confuse sitting taking notes with writing output you can sell!

What else can help you with culling tasks? Chapter 4 has several techniques for prioritizing and dropping to-dos. And when you feel especially stuck or undecided, remember that any decision is better than no decision. At least you are moving forward and learning. You can always change paths later, but if you stand rooted to the spot, you'll always see the same scenery.

One last tip for making tricky decisions: narrow it to two choices, and flip a coin. When it lands, your gut reaction will tell you what your heart believes is right.

Seeing Other Authors As Competition

Don't make the mistake of treating other authors like frenemies. In fact, far from being adversaries, they will probably be your strongest allies. Chapter 7 attempted to convince you of the value in building your tribe, so revisit that material if you still feel doubtful.

As Wendy Janes says, "Other authors can be companions not competitors."

You're highly unlikely to write fast enough that your readers only ever read your books (and how dull would that be for the literary landscape, anyway?), so the cross-promotional opportunities of teaming up with other authors are huge. Plus, they understand what you're going through, as they're experiencing many of the same struggles.

If you're on Goodreads, look at the current reading challenges being attempted and you'll see that many readers are enjoying a book a week, at least. There's plenty of demand and you can unquestionably afford to collaborate, not compete, with other authors.

Losing Your Work

The importance of backing up your book is widely known. You don't have to use a sophisticated system unless you want to: simply emailing your Work In Progress to yourself, or saving it to Google Drive, can suffice. This is part of my writing routine and I close every writing session with a backup. If you have extensive notes, research, or character sketches, you must back those up too.

You should also consider version control, where every few days (or every day if you are writing prolifically) you change the name of your document. If you start the filename with the date, you have the added bonus that your versions sort themselves easily too.

And don't forget to backup your website, especially if you are administering it yourself. If you don't know how to do this, either find out, or get someone to teach you. You should also take a few screenshots, just to remind yourself what you're aiming for, if the unthinkable happens to your online home. Regular updates will help keep your site safe, so don't neglect this easy task either.

Money Drains

It's theoretically possible to publish your book without spending a penny. But, I strongly advise that you don't! See Chapter 11 for key quality aspects to consider, and know that these items will, in all likelihood, call on your budget:
- Proofreading.
- Cover design.
- Interior formatting (unless you are technically adept with this).
- ISBN numbers.

However, unless you are able to spend money with abandon, you'll probably feel better about your results (profits) if you are cautious about expenditure. So where can you safely economize?

Best Areas to Save Money

Every author and every book is different and your circumstances will dictate where you need to spend money. However, these are the areas where I suggest you are especially cautious:

Developmental Editing

Unless you're truly trying to write Nobel Prize quality work, this is one area where you can educate yourself extensively.

There are tonnes of great books about plot construction, advice on culling scenes, character complexities, and so on. Don't simply write a mediocre book and then pay someone else to fix it. You're the author: this is your craft.

This is not to say you should attempt to fly entirely solo, but if you recruit a powerful beta reading team and/or find a critique partner you trust, you can spend time instead of dollars on polishing your book. If you're fairly competent, but simply too close to your own work, give it time to rest, or trade this service with another author.

And for goodness' sake, *read!* Find a sentence you don't like, and improve it. Pull out some classic children's books and see what you can learn from sentence structure and word choices. Go through a bestseller in your genre and mark the techniques the author has used. What's going on with action verbs, dialog tags, and adjectives? Are they distracting or do they flow nicely? Listen to a few audiobooks: do sentences sound clumsy, when read aloud?

Paid Promotions

Yes, you need to spend here, but spend *wisely*. Be especially clear on your goals for each promotion you're paying for. For example, do you want to:

- Reach new readers, and hope they'll read your books *someday*?
- Hit the *New York Times* Bestseller list, even if the promotion costs more than the extra books you sell?
- Deeply discount or give away one book, in the hope it causes a sale surge with other titles?
- Generate more in royalties than the promotion costs you?

Usually, when I run a promotion, I'm aiming for the last outcome. The others are still valid, if you're clear on what you're doing and why. With this goal in mind—and please know I have *not* tried every paid promotional channel for my fiction—of those I have used, at present I would only repeat BookBub and Ereader News Today. BookBub is an expensive investment but each time I've been featured, the gamble has more than paid off. Note that if you only have one published book, you might want to hold off from applying to BookBub until you have further titles available: the "halo" effect on other books can be significant.

Personally, I haven't had good results with any of the cheaper paid services. Other smaller promotions may only cost $10, but that isn't worth it to me if the resulting sales bump is minuscule. So, ask your tribe what works for them, and look for *recent* information from authors *in your genre* who understand the concept of Return on Investment. Many indie authors are surprisingly vague about the break-even number of sales they need.

Note that for fiction, it's highly unlikely to be worth your while hiring a professional publicist for your first novel. You simply won't see back the four-figure sum it costs you. (I'm not talking about a Virtual Assistant who will help nudge things along: I'm talking about a full-blown public relations service.) I talked with one indie author who had hired a publicist and I was alarmed to hear she had received, as part of the package, a list of bloggers whom she could contact for coverage. This is poor value: she, or a Virtual Assistant, could have spent 30 minutes on Google and compiled that list herself. Moreover, it was the publicist's job to reach out, not pass the work to the client. If you do decide to engage PR help, be clear on what services you'll receive.

Swag

Especially as a new author, you'll probably be so excited by your book's appearance in the world that you want to order some small book-related gifts. By all means, *do* splurge on bookmarks, postcards, mugs and fridge magnets, *if* they help you celebrate your indie success. Just know that costs can add up, and unless you have several live events on your calendar, you'll probably find yourself stuck with some of your swag. And I'm sorry to tell you that as a relatively unknown writer, readers will not get especially excited if you offer these items as prizes. Think about what *you* like to win and plan accordingly.

Giveaways

The last time I gave away paperbacks on Goodreads, I was pained by the results. I checked the reader profiles of several of my winners and the likelihood of them enjoying my novel was minimal. (My most obvious demographic is gender: my novels appeal overwhelmingly to women, not men.) And sure enough, after I sent the prizes, signed copies of my books promptly showed up on auction sites, suggesting that some readers were not entering to win for genuine reasons. It's incredibly distressing for an indie on a limited budget to pour money away like this.

Note that this was *before* Goodreads began charging authors to list giveaways—at the time of writing you can offer either print or Kindle format, and it will now cost upwards of $100—and you still have to buy and ship paperbacks, if those are your prize.

Instead, I'd suggest you offer free books to your newsletter subscribers, who have shown some loyalty and interest in your work already.

Offering prizes to attract new subscribers is also a popular tactic, and you may be able to craft a giveaway like this which works nicely for you. I recommend, however, that in your keenness to build your email list, you should avoid offering general prizes like Amazon credit. You'll risk landing dozens of fresh subscribers who are *only* chasing that prize: they have no interest in your books and are unlikely to stick around for the long term. Instead, try to craft a prize which only your targeted readers would actually enjoy, such as a collection of books in your genre.

The Gold Rush: One More Reminder About Money

Do you know who made the most money during California's Gold Rush? Not the miners, but the merchants who sold them their tools. This lesson is important for indie authors, because thousands of people are now charging serious money giving us advice on what to do. Some of them cite out of date or rare examples and then extract hundreds or thousands of dollars from us on the basis they can help us replicate improbable successes.

Keep in mind that if you spend, for example, $300 on a masterclass, you'll need to generate perhaps 200 additional book sales solely from what you learn, to cover the cost.

Avoid buying a service without researching if there's a free version which would meet your needs. It's reasonable, too, to ask the person recommending it if they're an affiliate, which means they earn a commission for signing you up. In the USA, the Federal Trade Commission requires this disclosure, and many other countries have equivalent rules.

Be extra wary of struggling authors who have rebranded themselves as editors or proofreaders. I recall one new error checker, who had plentiful mistakes in her own book! If you're thinking of hiring someone who has their own work for sale, pick up a copy and see if you're impressed.

Time Sucks

Try thinking of your time as a currency, and wasted time costs you lost words. For example, how many (first draft) words can you write in 30 minutes? That's your cost for being distracted by social media, procrastinating by cleaning the house, answering a call from a friend who wants to chat, and so on. Yes, it's vital to take breaks, but make sure they are intentional and refreshing, not just leaky time sucks.

Knowing where your time goes can be incredibly powerful. Laura Vanderkam, author of *168 Hours: You*

Have More Time Than You Think, advocates that you figure out exactly where your time goes. She cites the case of an incredibly busy woman whose water heater broke, taking up many hours of her week. Yet somehow, she found the time to deal with it. Vanderkam asks, if we can find that time when we must, how would it be to treat your priorities the same way?

Make sure you know your own personal time sucks, and do whatever you need to, to reduce or eliminate them. If you can't rely on willpower alone, sites like OmmWriter can be useful allies in protecting you from distractions.

Chapter 5 laid out tactics for making good use of time, and we've also covered avoiding email overload (Chapter 10) and the time cost of social media (Chapter 12). Below are some further time sucks which can be bad news for authors.

Obsessive Checking of Sales and Reviews

If you have a BookBub or other big promotion on your hands, you can be forgiven for endless refreshes of your book page to witness the giddying climb up through the sales rankings. However, for every other occasion, most indie authors do not need to check their sales figures more than about once a week, or even once a month. By all means do some analysis of how your books are selling and see what you can learn from it, but don't make it a daily or thrice-daily activity. It simply isn't meaningful and it distracts you from the real business at hand: writing and promoting.

The same goes for reviews from readers. By all means engage with your audience, but do it on your schedule. Aside from the time it takes, you risk having your day's writing derailed by an unkind review.

Trying to Be an Expert in the Amazon Algorithm

You do need to understand the basics of how Amazon chooses which books to show to people who are browsing their site. But it's not your job to be expert in this, and in any case, the "Zon bots" change their approach regularly. Instead, check in twice a year with wisdom shared by folks like David Gaughran, and see what key adjustments you might need to make. Amazon has legions of people and machines working on their highly sophisticated algorithms. You simply cannot afford to try to keep up.

Entering Writing Contests

Be careful when entering writing contests that the time it takes you to craft and submit an entry is worth it. Yes, it's a wonderful boost to the ego if you win or are shortlisted, and if your true goal is to impress an agent or land a traditional book deal, adding these accolades to your bio is a shrewd move. Equally, if your family and those you respect don't think you're a *real* writer because your work isn't at the front of their tiny village bookstore, winning something may help assure them of your competence.

But, for most indies, contests may not be worth your trouble, especially when you factor in entry fees. Be sure to keep an eye on the time involved and the results you're getting. If your readers love your work, they won't care about the prizes you've won. Otherwise, contests may fall into the category of busy-work, which doesn't actually contribute to your true productivity.

Giving Up Too Soon

This last pitfall is the biggest! Most of us indies have entertained a secret hope that we'd publish our first (or maybe second) book, rapidly attract a band of loyal fans who would rave about our work, and, within a few short weeks, end up with a bestseller on our hands and an interview slot on prime time TV, with movie rights to follow. After all, we can all name examples of authors who did just that, and if we can't, well-meaning friends take pains to send us articles of apparent overnight successes, whose royalties simply flooded in.

Well, all this is possible. It's wonderful, it's inspiring, and if it happens to you, hurrah. But I want you to know, it isn't likely, even if your book is mind-blowing. Breaking through as an indie author is staggeringly hard, even when you've done everything right. According to Bowker, in the USA, over a million books were published in 2016, around two-thirds of them by indies, while overall book sales are shrinking. Steven Piersanti of Berrett-Koehler Publishers reckons that any given book is competing with 13 million others available for sale.

While I've no wish to kill your dream altogether, I want you to know it's unlikely you'll find fame and fortune as an indie author. So, realize that if you're in this profession, you'd better be in it because you truly love it. If you would write for free, with book earnings as a delightful bonus, that might be a useful mindset to sustain you.

Or, you can think of it like Pat Edwards, who recalls the concept described by mythologist Joseph Campbell in his book, *The Hero With a Thousand Faces*. Edwards reminds us, "Realize you are on a Hero's Journey with your project. When you see your work as a Hero's Journey you know the stages and can set your expectations up accordingly. A Hero's Journey always starts out with our heroine as an ordinary person, living an ordinary life, but must now be brave enough to leave that ordinary-her behind and step into the fantastic."

Also know that if you do find a degree of success, studies have shown this tends to occur only *after* you have a few books out there. Indie author earnings are strongly correlated with the number of books the author has published. So, you need to be in it for the longer term: publishing a couple of books and then giving up is an understandable but lamentable pitfall. However, author fatigue is a very real problem, and is one of the prime reasons I began writing this book.

My best advice: pace yourself and bring snacks.

Summary

In any business, it takes time to find your own path. However, I hope that by knowing some of the most common author pitfalls, your journey becomes a little quicker, smoother, and more enjoyable. Focus on steady progress and be mindful of both your time and money. Take every reasonable step to safeguard your mental energy for the main purpose: writing your book.

And remember, towering above all the factors discussed in this chapter: the biggest threat to your indie author career is you deciding to give up.

Self-Reflection Questions

1) If you've already set a date for your first or next book publication, how would it feel to give yourself a few extra weeks?

2) Where in your author business have you recently spent money which did not bring a worthwhile return?

3) Can you identify at least one activity which is currently taking your time, which you could reduce or eliminate?

Chapter 14: Things Not to Worry About

One of the principles I've stressed already in this book is that with only limited time and mental bandwidth as an indie author, you can't possibly do everything. Nor should you worry about every potential issue which crosses your path. If you spend time online connecting with other authors (as almost all of us do), you're especially likely to be drawn into anxiety-inducing conversations. If you're not careful, some of these topics become not only a huge time suck, but they can distract you from the true business at hand: your writing.

Of course, it's up to you what you feel is truly important and what you decide is worth your worry. Just be sure you're being intentional, before you get drawn into spending energy on an issue.

I've listed below the things I recommend you choose not to worry about.

Piracy

The idea of someone stealing your precious work, and the hours of effort it represents, is a scary thing when you first encounter it. If you've set up a Google Alert for your name and/or book title, from time to time you will get notifications which appear to suggest your book is available online, free to download, from channels you haven't authorized.

First, keep in mind some of these sites and links do not actually contain your work; they have been created as "click bait" to attract new consumers and harvest personal information. But even if your book *is* available to download, you have to decide whether as a lone author you have the inclination and stamina to tackle what are often sophisticated criminal outlets, typically operating overseas. Unless you have a background in copyright enforcement, I'd suggest the time, money, and grief it would cause you to go after these sites simply isn't worth it.

Moreover, there is a credible school of thought which suggests if these readers didn't get your work for free, they wouldn't become paying customers anyway. Seth Godin, who's written 18 books, is clear on where your worries should lie: "The enemy of an author is not piracy, but obscurity."

To clarify, if someone clones your whole book, changes the title and cover, and uploads it to a mainstream retailer like Amazon or Barnes & Noble as though it were their own, that's an infringement I'd consider worth pursuing through the retailer's help channels.

Amazon's Profits

As an indie author, the chances are sky-high that you sell, or intend to sell, your books on Amazon. So the earlier you can make your peace with this fact, the better: Amazon is a for-profit business. It has shareholders to satisfy and long-term growth goals. It is not there to support your writing career and, frankly, it doesn't owe you much. It can, and will, change its rules, royalties, algorithms, and processes to benefit itself, not you.

If you choose to grant exclusive rights to your ebooks through a program like KDP Select, you need to go into that with your eyes open and know that you may indeed be helping Amazon reach a position of market domination which could obliterate other booksellers. And if you choose not to give it exclusive rights, you have to determine whether you are damaging your sales to the extent where your own indie author career is in jeopardy. At the time of writing, I have three of my four books enrolled in KDP Select and I know I'm helping to create a landscape I don't welcome. That's a decision I've made and I live with it.

That said, you may choose to invest a *judicious* amount of time (see section entitled *Time Sucks* in Chapter 13) in understanding Amazon's visibility algorithm, to keep your book information targeted and help readers find your work. Because Amazon is in business for profit, it will show its website visitors the books likely to result in the highest profits for them. That means books likely to sell in high numbers, at great profit margins, get top position in Amazon's typical search results. So until you're a raging success, Amazon won't do much to help people see your books… which of course means you don't become a raging success. The takeaway here is that if you don't want to sink without trace on Amazon's virtual shelves, you'll need to light your own fire under your book sales.

Know also that there are other villains in this plot. Amazon is in the long tail game of publishing indie authors, by which I mean it makes tiny amounts of money from many, many vendors. As such, its processes are necessarily highly automated: it simply cannot afford human oversight of every title listed for sale. Many unscrupulous "authors" spend considerable time trying to game the Amazon algorithm, particularly in respect to royalty payouts. As a result, from time to time Amazon announces sweeping new rules, often accompanied by seemingly draconian crackdowns on offenders. Some of the offenders are innocent authors who have appeared as a false positive in Amazon's efforts to clean up the game. For these authors, the consequences can be extremely damaging and distressing, and if you look for them, you can find plenty of outrage among online author communities.

I'm not trying to belittle these experiences but my advice, for your sanity, is to try to avoid worrying about these episodes until you are directly affected. In the meantime, know that it isn't fair and it isn't pretty. Just keep writing.

Social Media Charges

While we're on the topic of big players being in business to make money, please remember the same thing applies to Facebook, LinkedIn, Instagram, and every other "free" channel which you may have become accustomed to using to connect with your readers. Once you have built up a following, these companies are entirely within their rights to start to charge you to talk to your fans. Not only is it possible they'll want your money, it's probable.

The antidote, as many in our industry have been saying for years, is to make sure you collect email addresses and gain permission from your readers to talk to them directly. If you're a heavy social media user yourself, setting up an email distribution list may feel like a hard slog by comparison. And there's no denying the value in talking to your readers where they happen to hang out all the time. But that does leave you open to a change in policy from your favorite social platform. Direct ownership of email addresses is a much less risky path, and Chapter 12 will get you started.

Being Outed As an Indie

One of my strongest recommendations for indie authors is that you make peace with the fact you *are* independent. See Chapter 3, if you still aren't quite comfortable with this choice. The industry is changing: "indie" no longer has the stigma once attached to "vanity publishing" and any negative aura that does exist is mainly in the mind of those who work in traditional publishing.

While it's no fun to be seen as second best, do remember Eleanor Roosevelt's famous advice that no one can actually make you feel inferior without your consent. So, you can save yourself a lot of energy by not worrying about people finding out you're an indie author. Believe me, if your readers love you, they don't care how you reach their bookshelf or device.

Once you own the *indie* tag proudly, you won't expend too much effort on forming your own publishing imprint so that your Amazon listing page doesn't betray you. Nor will you put yourself through heartache wondering if the ISBN number on the back of your paperback is telling tales. Truly, these are *not* the factors which will make or break your indie author career. If you find yourself unduly concerned about being outed as an indie, you're probably not fully committed to this publishing model.

Negative Reviews

Let's look, though, at what readers do care about and how they can ruin your day in other ways. The most obvious peril is negative reviews. I'm not going to lie: harsh reviews hurt. Depending how many total online reviews you have, they may sting a little, or they may slash a bleeding hole in your chest. But you mustn't allow negative reader feedback to bring your scribbling to a halt or crush your fragile writer's confidence.

Yes, you can learn from constructive comments, especially if readers are helpful enough to be specific. And be sure to take note of reviews about key quality factors, like typos, formatting or inconsistencies between what your product promised and what you delivered.

However, more often than not, a negative review is simply a sign that you didn't find your ideal reader on that occasion. If you get a cluster of them, you might want to revisit your cover and your blurb, since somewhere between the purchase decision and the end of the book, you fell short in meeting your end of the bargain.

Otherwise, think of three of your all-time favorite books and look at the one- and two-star online reviews. You'll find there is no such thing as a book which delights every reader. And nor should there be. Just focus on finding your ideal audience and giving that niche readership the book that sends *them* into raptures.

Reviews Which Are Simply Wrong

More frustrating than a negative review is one where the reader makes a statement which you know is unequivocally wrong. To date, all my novels have been set in England, yet one reviewer (who was fairly positive) made a point of mentioning how much they love fiction that takes place in Ireland. Sorry, but that's a 300-mile difference, which is a big deal in Europe. In another amusing example, a reviewer was charmed by the illustrations of teacups in my books. Again, tea and cake play a cheerful part in my narrative, but (unless she drew them herself) there are no pictures in any of my novels.

What do you do with these reviews? Just follow the rock-solid advice which is the foundation of your sanity: let them be. Ignore them. Don't respond online, don't defend your writing, don't correct the misperception, and don't get into any back and forth. There are plenty of horror stories of authors who did try to engage in review tennis, and, apart from the time and sleep they surely lost, their reputations were only harmed by doing so. If you are lucky enough to have loyal readers who will step in on your behalf, that's great, but please get out of their way.

The sole exception I'd grant here is for the memorable scenario related by Jackie Bouchard, who did once respond to an inaccurate posting: "A woman said in an Amazon review that she'd loved the book but was 'sorry to hear that the author recently died'!"

Aside from disproving reports of your early demise, please, have no part in any review rebuttal.

Reviews with Spoilers

Some authors get agitated when readers leave reviews which contain plot spoilers, fearing this ruins the experience for other buyers. Sadly these overenthusiastic summaries are inevitable, and hopefully they make up only a minority of your total reviews. You can comfort yourself that, with luck, most readers won't see them.

Boomerang Buyers

A boomerang buyer is someone who purchases your book, and quickly returns it for a refund. Possibly, they read it in the interim. Possibly, they didn't. You can't know, and grimacing like you're sucking on a lemon won't help you feel better about it. Some people are cheap. They think saving $3.99, or less, is a great game and they don't hesitate to play it, at your expense. But, hopefully, these are a minority of your readers, and it's unlikely these folk will become your superfans in any case.

And do keep in mind the possibility that someone made a genuine purchasing mistake: I've certainly done it, by clicking too fast and buying the wrong title by the same author.

Objectionable though it may be, boomerang buying is simply another customer quirk you'll have to shrug off.

Unsubscribers

Let's say you have an email newsletter—well done—and possibly even some free content (also known as a lead magnet) to encourage people to sign up—even better! You'll need to get used to the fact that every time you send out a communication to your list, people will unsubscribe. You can lessen the pain of this by disabling the notification which cheerfully announces their leaving. If you're extremely analytical, you might be tempted to deduce what you wrote which led to a mass desertion, but in general I don't think such soul-searching is worth it.

You can also try to be pleased about people who leave your list. Personally, I'm ferocious about unsubscribing: it keeps my email inbox under control, which is a big factor in my sanity and having the mental bandwidth to actually *write*. And I'm almost evangelical in encouraging others to unsubscribe from emails they don't enjoy receiving (see Chapter 10). As a reader, life is simply too short to plow through content which doesn't excite you. And as a sender, it's the equivalent of going to a party where nobody welcomes your presence: why would you put yourself through that?

Instead, whenever someone unsubscribes from your list, work toward being happy for them. They just regained a little of their own sanity. And, for you, the average engagement of the people you're talking to just increased.

Great Problems to Have

Try not to spend more than a few seconds worrying about things which would, in fact, be great problems to have. At one point I entered a writing contest and the prize was an unusual type of book contract, with a big player. I found myself hypothesizing over whether that would be a strategically limiting outcome for me. In truth, this would have been a *terrific* problem to have.

I also heard from an indie author who had resisted setting up an email newsletter with MailChimp, as it might be a relatively pricey option once she reached 2000 subscribers. Guess what: if you muster this many readers who are longing to hear about your books, you have a pretty great problem. Paying to reach them is unlikely to be your top worry, and if the charges do seem too cumbersome, you can invest your previous savings in paying for help to switch providers. In this example, the author had chosen a service she thought was better value, which had then gone out of business. The chafing result: she still had no one on her mailing list at all.

In other words, don't cross bridges before you get there. Don't worry about things which *might* cost you money in the future, if they accompany the case where you'd be selling cartloads of books.

Summary

As an indie author you're wearing so many hats, and caring about so many details, that purposefully deciding there are some things you will *not* worry about is the only sustainable choice. While it's an individual process to determine the niggles that are, in fact, important to you, I strongly suggest that if you're going to experience anxiety around publishing, it should be directed toward factors *you* control.

Focus your worries on things that are likely to happen and would have a significant impact, and try not to get too hung up on the profit strategies of the big guns, or shady behavior of smaller players.

Self-Reflection Questions

1) Have you felt anxiety around any of the topics mentioned in this chapter?

2) Are there any aspects you now feel you can add to your list of "Things I Won't Worry About"? If there are, write them down and keep your list somewhere you'll see it often.

Chapter 15: Keeping Your Spirits Up

Poets, comedians, business tycoons, and philanthropists have similar things to say about overnight success: it can take 15 to 20 years. In his book *The Juggling Author*, Jim Heskett warns, "A lot of challenging times will come before succeeding... don't expect that you won't struggle."

We've already established that the biggest single threat to your indie author career is you deciding to give up. If you think about it, that's a great position to be in—traditionally published authors face more external threats, as they have so much less control over getting their writing in front of readers.

However, just because your biggest peril is internal doesn't mean it's not significant. As well as all the other tasks you have to juggle as an indie author, you're also Chief Morale Officer for your business. Here are some ways to take care of that responsibility.

Celebrate Success

Hopefully it goes without saying that when you publish a book, you should pop open the bubbly, dance on the table, fling your hat off a cliff, or whatever else "celebrate" means to you. But don't forget to pat yourself on the back for smaller moments, too. Tracey Gemmell agrees: "Celebrate every achievement, from publishing the first book to finally understanding the difference between an en and an em dash. These breakthroughs will carry you through the crash and burns."

When you start consciously looking for milestones to celebrate, you'll notice more and more of them. They might feel big, like a completed first draft, sending a book to beta readers, or reaching your first five online reviews. Even small successes like achieving your daily word count goal, or consistently showing up to write, are worthy of note. Thousands of people *claim* they want to write a book: you're *doing it*, so take a bow.

Make a Happy File

A Happy File is a useful way of capturing and acknowledging small successes, and is a particularly nourishing habit. This is simply a place, either physical or electronic, where you gather every small piece of good news or writing achievement.

To start, ask yourself whether you want to make a simple list, or whether you'd like a more visual record, with pictures. Decide whether you want to make a physical Happy File (on paper, as a list or scrapbook) or electronic (for example, a Word document or on Pinterest).

Author Heather Wardell sees her Happy File whenever she pauses her writing: "My computer screensaver is a series of pictures of positive comments people have made about my books. So whenever I stop working for too long, my computer starts showing me exactly why my writing matters, how it's helped people and brought them enjoyment."

So, get gathering! Anything which makes you feel good about your writing can go in your file. For example:
- A complimentary email from a reader
- A positive online review
- The word count of your Work In Progress
- Launch party photos
- Your sales rank during a promotion
- Your book cover image(s)
- A feature about you, either online or in print media
- Photos of you meeting readers in person

Make a regular date with yourself to add to your Happy File, and you might be pleasantly surprised how fast it builds. Then, on days when the doldrums descend, call on your file and enjoy the lift it brings.

Lean on Your Support Network

Feeling stuck? Tempted to give up before you publish? Crushed by a critical review? These are all ideal times to lean on your support network.

Hopefully, you've already banked some karma by supporting other authors, encouraging them, and reading/reviewing their work. (See Chapter 7.) If you have, your writer tribe will be there for you when you get a little down. If your recent author earnings were only enough for a cup of coffee, your peeps will confirm they've had times like that too. If the review you just read makes you want to throw up, check with your buddies for confirmation they've all experienced that sickening lurch from tough feedback.

Clearly, you don't want to be the kind of author who joins an online (or real) group simply to whine about how hard this writing lark is. Like any relationship, you'll aim to show up in a positive mood most of the time. But once you've established some strong writing friendships, don't be afraid to be vulnerable sometimes. Not only can writing be lonely, it can be tough too. When you need a hug, your tribe will offer it, and perhaps even wrap you in a metaphorical fluffy blanket.

In Chapter 2, you also identified friends and family members who may not know much about writing, but still believe in you and your abilities. Be intentional about spending time with these upbeat people when you need a boost. You'll find this also helps add perspective about your writerly woes. Chances are, you have acquaintances who are going through their own, potentially serious, challenges. Make time to connect meaningfully with them, offer what assistance you can, and you'll likely find your own troubles seem a little less burdensome.

Avoid Absolute Thinking

Catching your thoughts is a powerful benefit of a meditation practice (see Chapter 8) and a key reason I'm eager for you to try it.
Do messages like these ever cross your mind?
- "My work is completely useless."
- "I'll never get this book finished."
- "No one will read this anyway..."
- "This always happens to me..."

If so, you're probably stumbling into absolute thinking, which means you're not only seeing things purely in black and white, but probably the negative side too.
Instead, try to reframe your thoughts and notice how your ease improves:
- "This manuscript needs considerable work before it's ready for readers."
- "I've not written much this week, but I'm still making overall progress."
- "My work might only have niche appeal, but it's important to me to share my message."
- "That was rotten luck, but I can do x and y to get back on track."

You can develop the skill of noticing your absolute thinking and then challenging those thoughts. In doing so, you're not only being kinder to yourself, but more realistic too. Things are rarely as bad as our inner voice would have us believe.

Decline to Compare

It's tempting, especially when you're still finding your feet as an author, to look around you at how others are doing. And it can be informative, if you approach comparisons with an inquisitive, learning mindset. After all, you can glean a tonne of good information from how other authors are running their businesses and how they're promoting their work to readers.

The trouble is that objective analysis can quickly slide into self-criticism. You can rapidly become discouraged and feel your work, or your results, (or both) don't measure up. You can always find an author who is more prolific and more successful than you. From there, doubt and negativity can set in fast, and before long, as Theodore Roosevelt famously said, comparison becomes the "thief of joy."

Try to remember the following:
- Most of us present a positive spin on facts to the outside world. Don't compare your insides to someone else's outsides. (That last sentence is a quote attributed to Rob Lowe, Anne Lamott, and others.)
- In particular, don't compare your first draft to their last draft.
- Chances are, the other authors you're looking at have been in the business longer, or have more time to devote to their efforts. It can be extremely off-putting to see others publishing a book every three or four months, when it takes you three or four years.
- Everyone—*everyone*—has setbacks and doubts.

In his memoir *What I Talk About When I Talk About Running*, Haruki Murakami says, "In the novelist's profession, as far as I'm concerned, there's no such thing as winning or losing... What's crucial is whether your writing attains the standards you've set for yourself."

Take a Sabbatical From Your Writing

If all else fails, it's perfectly okay to take a pause from your writing for a while. Sometimes, when your creative tank is empty and your motivation hits zero, you just need to regroup. Review the information on taking a break or a short retreat (Chapter 8) but know that if this doesn't feel enough, a longer absence from your writing is *not* the same as giving up.

Since the best sabbaticals are both restful and inspiring, here are my top suggestions for what to do with your time:
- Reread books you adored from your childhood. You'll probably fall in love with them all over again.
- Get curious. Pick a topic you know nothing about and see if you can learn the basics. If the news is full of something which confuses you, dig into it.
- Travel, especially to a new culture. Even a shorter trip will almost certainly awaken your senses and offer fresh inspiration. But don't try to force your enthusiasm, just observe your surroundings and go with the flow.
- Thank someone who's been supportive of your writing efforts and quirky moods. Repay a few favors, or throw yourself into something they've been hoping to do together with you.

Clearly, a writing sabbatical is a great opportunity to undertake a significant volunteer project (see above). You could also combine this with travel, or being with friends. In addition, many of the self-care ideas from Chapter 8 work well during sabbaticals too:
- You might now have bandwidth to try a tangential hobby that's new to you, or pick up something you used to enjoy.
- Even if you've been taking regular exercise, your sabbatical gives you the freedom to aim further or faster. If you're not writing, you might enjoy a

challenging goal like a long-distance hike, or training for a 5K race.
- Spend quality time with friends, particularly those who don't write.

You don't need to set a duration for your sabbatical, just play it by ear. You'll know when you're ready to pick up your pen again.

Give Back to the Writing Community

I recently talked with a writer who is juggling a full-time job and kids alongside her author aspirations. There's nothing unusual in that, but she had concluded that she simply doesn't have time to help other writers at present. I can see how one would reach that belief, but I couldn't disagree more.

Not only is it a wonderful thing to support other authors, but you will reap the rewards from the effort you put in many times over. And, assuming you read for pleasure in any case (hello, you're a writer!), then it doesn't have to be especially time consuming.

Chapter 7 encouraged you to build your writing tribe, but at times when you feel especially low, putting in some extra effort to give back to the community can result in a significant morale boost for you as well.

Finally, you should look at giving back to your wider community too. Author Tracey Gemmell has found a fitting way to do this. She says, "While receiving little or no income, consider volunteering. I find it eases my guilt at being 'kept' while establishing my writing business. I tutor refugees in English. Great use of a writer's language skills!"

Do More of the Parts You Love

Unless you're a true chameleon, the chances are high that there are parts of the writing and publishing process you love more than others. You may have encountered some tasks which were so enjoyable they didn't feel like work, where other parts felt like sheer torture.

When your spirits take a dip, make a conscious switch to spend time on the parts you love, even if that means swapping projects. For example, if the first draft ignites your enthusiasm, take a few days to work on something entirely new, even if you haven't finished your current Work In Progress. But do set some boundaries on this, otherwise you'll fall into the tempting creative trap of having project fragments littering your life like confetti.

For Martha Reynolds, the editing phase is more appealing. "I do enjoy the editing process, much more than getting that crappy first draft done. Fine-tuning my words and phrases, adding layers to my characters, tweaking dialogue—it's all fun, especially when I'm not on a deadline."

Even when your morale is not flagging, being aware of the parts you dislike is useful. If they're not related to the core writing, outsource pesky tasks to someone else as soon as you can justify it. Freeing yourself up for what you love and do best is a sound investment.

Cat Lavoie simply aims to keep moving forward. She says, "I try to focus on writing my next story, improving my craft, and learning about the business. And I try to have fun while I'm doing it."

Finally, take a look back at what is most important to you (Chapter 3). Divert some time and effort toward this outcome and when you pull it off, you'll receive a disproportionate boost. And if you're not quite at the point where your proudest accomplishment is possible, you can concoct something similar. For example, are you still writing, but yearn to hold your book in your hands? Print out your mocked-up cover and admire it anyway. Perhaps you're still editing, but excited about a signing in a bookstore? Maybe you can offer a talk on being a writer instead. Give yourself a taste of your treasured prize as early as you can.

Self-Reflection Questions

1) What format will you choose for your Happy File? Can you think of five small successes to add to it? Start your file today.

2) Are you making good use of your support network? Is there someone you could reach out to this week?

3) Which parts of the writing process do you love, and how could you spend a little more time on these?

Conclusion

The joy of publishing independently and being in charge of our author destiny brings an obligation to play many roles and juggle a plethora of tasks. What's more, the self-reliant, motivated personality traits which make us well suited to the independent route are also the parts of our character which can cause us to take on too much, criticize ourselves, neglect our own well-being, and eventually crumple under stress.

I hope this book has shown that knowing yourself, working with mindful productivity, and being diligent about caring for yourself and your creativity are the foundations to an enjoyable, long-term indie author career. We identified your strengths and support mechanisms, and examined your goals and how to stay focused on them. We looked at building both your craft and your tribe, and the many options you have for cultivating a balanced, creative lifestyle. Finally, we looked at pitfalls to dodge and worries you can afford to rebuff.

It's my sincere wish to leave you feeling both positive and purposeful about your writing business, and that you are now better equipped to approach your indie author journey with a sense of ease.

Download free bonus materials here:
www.paulinewiles.com/indie-with-ease-bonus
And find me at:
www.paulinewiles.com

Finally, please consider adding your review of *Indie With Ease* to the site where you purchased this book, Goodreads, and other online forums.

Resources

As well as the authors who contributed to this book, the following writers were mentioned:

Rachel Aaron, http://rachelaaron.net/
Bella Andre, http://bellaandre.com/
Claire Cook, http://clairecook.com/
Jim Heskett, http://www.jimheskett.com/
Guy Kawasaki, https://guykawasaki.com/
Kim Manganelli, https://wisteriawriters.com/
Lisa Manterfield, http://lisamanterfield.com/
Haruki Murakami, http://www.harukimurakami.com/
Gretchen Rubin, https://gretchenrubin.com/

Website References

The Four Tendencies Quiz
https://gretchenrubin.com/take-the-quiz

85K Writing Challenge
https://85k90.com/

Agendio planners (affiliate link)
https://agendio.com/referrals-welcome/wpzCLW_1507566620

Association of American Publishers
https://publishers.org/

Author Earnings
http://authorearnings.com/

Bates Method International
http://seeing.org/

Berrett-Koehler's blog
https://www.bkconnection.com/the-10-awful-truths-about-book-publishing

BookBub
https://www.bookbub.com

BookMap
http://bookmap.org

Buffer
https://buffer.com

Calm
https://www.calm.com/

David Gaughran
http://davidgaughran.com/

Ereader News Today
https://ereadernewstoday.com/

Fiverr
https://www.fiverr.com/

Flying Wish Paper
https://www.flyingwishpaper.com/

Goodreads
https://www.goodreads.com/

Happier Podcast
https://gretchenrubin.com/podcasts/

Media Bistro
https://www.mediabistro.com/

Mindfulness Interview with Mark Abramson
https://bewell.stanford.edu/mindfulness-and-meditation/

National Novel Writing Month
http://nanowrimo.org

OmmWriter
https://ommwriter.com/

Pomodoro technique
https://en.wikipedia.org/wiki/Pomodoro_Technique

Recurpost
https://recurpost.com/

Scrivener
https://www.literatureandlatte.com/scrivener/overview

Self-Compassion
http://self-compassion.org/

Self-Publishing Advice Conference
http://selfpublishingadviceconference.com/

Self-Pub Boot Camp
http://selfpubbootcamp.com

She Writes Press
https://shewritespress.com

Smashwords
https://www.smashwords.com/

The Book Designer Cover Awards
https://www.thebookdesigner.com/2011/08/monthly-e-book-cover-design-awards/

Wattpad
https://www.wattpad.com/

Wix
https://www.wix.com/

Bibliography

Aaron, Rachel. *2k to 10k: Writing Faster, Writing Better, and Writing More of What You Love.* CreateSpace Independent Publishing, 2017.
Addey, Melissa. *100 Things to Do While Breastfeeding.* Letterpress Publishing, 2015.
Alderson, Martha. *The Plot Whisperer.* Adams Media, 2011.
Baty, Chris. *No Plot? No Problem!* Chronicle Books, 2014.
Brantmark, Niki. *Lagom: Not Too Little, Not Too Much: The Swedish Art of Living a Balanced, Happy Life.* Harper Design, 2017.
Cain, Susan. *Quiet: The Power of Introverts in a World That Can't Stop Talking.* Broadway Books, 2013.
Cameron, Julia. *The Artists' Way.* TarcherPerigee, 2016.
Campbell, Joseph. *The Hero With a Thousand Faces (The Collected Works of Joseph Campbell).* New World Library, 2008.
Corbett, David. *The Art of Character.* Penguin Books, 2013.
Currey, Mason. *Daily Rituals: How Artists Work.* Knopf, 2013.
Ducie, Elizabeth. *The Business of Writing.* Chudleigh Phoenix Publications, 2018.
Hale, Constance. *Vex, Hex, Smash, Smooch.* W. W. Norton & Company, 2013.

Henry, Todd. *Die Empty: Unleash Your Best Work Every Day*. Portfolio, 2015.
Heskett, Jim. *The Juggling Author: How To Write Four Books a Year While Balancing Family, Friends, and a Full-Time Job*. Royal Arch Books, 2017.
Huffington, Arianna. *The Sleep Revolution: Transforming Your Life, One Night at a Time*. Harmony, 2017.
King, Carla. *A Consumer's Guide for Self-Publishers: Writing & Publishing Tools and Services*. Misadventures Media, 2018.
Lamott, Anne. *Bird by Bird: Some Instructions on Writing and Life*. Anchor, 1995.
Mammen, George and Guy Faulkner. "Physical Activity and the Prevention of Depression: A Systematic Review of Prospective Studies," *American Journal of Preventive Medicine* Vol. 45, No. 5, 2013.
Mohr, Tara. *Playing Big*. Avery, 2014.
Moore, Dinty W. *The Mindful Writer; Noble Truths of the Writing Life*. Wisdom Publications, 2016.
Moran, Brian P. and Michael Lennington. *The 12 Week Year: Get More Done in 12 Weeks than Others Do in 12 Months*. Wiley, 2013.
Murakami, Haruki. *What I Talk About When I Talk About Running*. Vintage, 2009.
Oppezzo, Marily and Daniel L. Schwartz. "Give Your Ideas Some Legs: The Positive Effect of Walking on Creative Thinking," *Journal of Experimental Psychology* Vol. 40, No. 4, 2014.
Rhimes, Shonda. *The Year of Yes*. Simon & Schuster, 2016.
Rubin, Gretchen. *The Four Tendencies*. Harmony, 2017.
Soojung-Kim Pang, Alex. *Rest: Why You Get More Done When You Work Less*. Basic Books, 2016.
Vanderkam, Laura. *168 Hours: You Have More Time Than You Think*. Portfolio, 2011.

Bonus Downloads

Find these here:
www.paulinewiles.com/indie-with-ease-bonus

- Self-reflection workbook
- Writing tracker
- Weekly time planner
- Quadrant chart (blank)
- Quadrant chart (completed example)
- Self-care tracker
- Templates from my work:
  - List of superfluous words to cut
  - Questions for beta readers (fiction and nonfiction)
  - Review request example (*Saving Saffron Sweeting*)
  - My filing structure
  - Checklists
    - Title announcement and pre-order phase
    - Reviewing a printed proof
    - Pre-launch and launch phases

Free Mini Course: Focus for Writers

To receive my free mini course,
Focus for Writers, visit:

www.paulinewiles.com/writers/focus-for-writers/

www.ingramcontent.com/pod-product-compliance
Lightning Source LLC
Chambersburg PA
CBHW050638300426
44112CB00012B/1843